THE ROMANCE OF THE BIBLE

THE ROMANCE OF THE BIBLE

By CHARLES J. E. KINGSTON

Author of
"The Coming of Christ—and After"

PICKERING & INGLIS Ltd.

LONDON, GLASGOW, MANCHESTER, LIVERPOOL, EDINBURGH

First Published in October, 1938

PREFACE

IN writing the story of the Bible it has been the author's object to show to his readers a little of the romance with which its history has been surrounded. None can be more conscious of defects in its presentation than is the author himself, and for these he would crave his readers' indulgence. For it he makes no claims of literary beauty; his object has always been to present facts as clearly, and as interestingly, as possible.

In September, 1538, there was issued, with all the authority of a royal proclamation, an order that all clergy should provide, before a specified date, " one boke of the whole Bible, in the largest volume, in Englyshe, sett up in summe convenyent place within the churche that ye have cure of, whereat your parishioners may most commodiously resort to the same and rede yt."

In April, 1539, the first edition of the Great Bible, a magnificent specimen of the art of printing in that day, was ready for publication. It at once took rank as the " authorised version " of its time, and so the battle of the English Bible was finally won. " First forbidden; then silently tolerated; and next licensed, it was now commanded by the King's Highness to be set up for the benefit of each one of the eleven thousand parishes in the land."

In these days, however, 400 years later, the battle has to be fought again. Not now against persecution, but against that Higher Criticism and Modernism which would steal our heritage from us and, above all, against that indifference which would leave the Bible to moulder on the damp shelves of carelessness.

If this book should arouse some to read the Bible more frequently, and to love it more ardently, and to listen to its message more thoughtfully, then the author will be well repaid for any work entailed in its preparation. He would desire, also, to acknowledge help received from the writings of others, to most of whom acknowledgments have been made in the footnotes. To any inadvertently overlooked, he would offer his sincere apologies and admit his indebtedness.

To the Holy Spirit, the Author of the best Book of all, are these pages reverently dedicated. Amen.

CONTENTS

The Romance of the Bible

CHAPTER I

HOW THE SCRIPTURES WERE GIVEN

IN studying the Bible we must remember that it is especially an Eastern book and that many of its passages can only be fully understood when the Eastern customs are known. It will be our purpose in these chapters to endeavour to throw light upon many of these misunderstood verses. One day when visiting the British Museum I had the opportunity of a few moments' conversation with one of the official lecturers there. He said to me, " The Bible does not so much need defending as explaining." C. H. Spurgeon said something very similar. " There is no need to defend the Bible. One does not defend a lion; let it out of its cage, and it will defend itself !"

Do you ask, " How was the Bible given?" Peter answers that question in his Epistle (II. Pet. i. 21) when he says, " Prophecy came not in old time by the will of man : but holy men of God spake as they were moved by the Holy Ghost." The Greek word *pheromenoi* translated " moved " means borne or carried. It is the same word that Jesus uses in John xv. 4, " As the branch cannot bear fruit of itself, except it abide in the vine; no more can ye, except ye abide in Me." Just as it was necessary for the sap to go through the branch before it could bear fruit so the Holy Spirit had to move upon the minds and hearts of the writers of the Scriptures before the

1

divine fruit of God's Word, which is so sweet to our taste, could be borne.

The same word is used to describe the wind that blew upon the disciples on the Day of Pentecost (Acts ii. 2). Here it is rendered " rushing." What grander word could describe the mighty impulse that thrilled the writers of the Scriptures as they penned its pages than this same " rushing mighty wind "?

Christ in John xxi. 18 uses this same word to show Peter how that in his old age " another shall gird thee, and carry thee whither thou wouldest not." Here the thought is of an outside power which controls the movements of Peter. In such a manner the Holy Spirit controlled the writers of the Scriptures so that they were preserved from error in that which they wrote.

Paul (II. Tim. iii. 16) brings out the same thought when he says "All scripture is given by inspiration of God . . . " Here the Greek word is *Theopneustos* which means " God-breathed." If one breathes upon the window on a frosty day, immediately a most beautiful floral design is formed by the frost. God breathed through man the beautiful design and plan of His revelation. Of course the human writers left the stamp of their own personality upon the outward form of their writings, just as it is conceivable that Christ, who is the Living Word, and who was conceived of the Holy Ghost, although born of the virgin Mary, bore some resemblance in features to His mother, Mary. Yet, just as Christ was divine as well as human, so the written Word of God bears the marks of the human channels through which it was given, while still remaining the divine Word. The poetry of David is different from the proverbs of Solomon; the logic of Paul differs from the serenity of John. Yet through all breathes the Spirit of God. An early Christian writer illustrates this thus: " One and the same rain comes down on all the world; yet it becomes white in the lily, red in the rose, purple in the violet and pansy. . . . It is uniform and changes not, but by adapting itself to the nature of each thing that receives it, it becomes what is appropriate to each."

The actual words of the Scriptures were inspired so that the writers were preserved from error in that which they wrote while under inspiration. Thus there was not a mechanical dictation on the part of God corresponding to that of an office manager to his stenographer; rather God used the individuality of each writer and yet preserved that which was written from error.

In proof of this consider the marvellous care bestowed by Him on the minute things of His creation. The finest needle of human manufacture under a microscope appears as a coarse, rusty, pock-marked poker while the needles of God's making, the thorn or the sting of the wasp, if examined, show a fine point no matter how high the power of the magnification. In all things " His work is perfect " (Deut. xxxii. 4) and if in the minute things God has exercised such care, then surely in such an important thing as His revelation of Himself we may expect as much or more.

Indeed, the Scripture writers themselves claim this verbal inspiration as the passages given below will prove:

" And Moses wrote all the words of the Lord " (Exod. xxiv. 4).

" The Spirit of the Lord spake by me, and His word was in my tongue " (II. Sam. xxiii. 2).

" The Lord said unto me, Behold I have put My words in thy mouth " (Jer. i. 9).

Paul said, " Which things also we speak, not in the words which man's wisdom teacheth, but which the Holy Ghost teacheth " (I. Cor. ii. 13).

Indeed, in the New Testament there are 284 quotations from the Old Testament, and these quotations are repeatedly prefaced by the words " It is written " in indication of full and final authority.

It is noteworthy, too, that the writers attached great importance to the very words used in Scripture. In proof of this note how Paul, writing to the Galatians (iii. 16) proves the necessity of simple faith in Christ by calling attention to the use of the singular " Seed " instead of the plural word " seeds." Again, the writer to the Hebrews (xii. 27) elaborates an important argument concerning the final judgment from the use, by the Prophet from whom he quotes the passage (Hag. ii. 6), of the words " Yet once more." Christ, from the Old Testament, proved to the Sadducees the doctrine of the resurrection in these words, " Now that the dead are raised even Moses shewed at the bush, when he calleth the Lord the God of Abraham, and the God of Isaac, and the God of Jacob " (Luke xx. 37). Indeed, Christ gave the whole weight of His authority to the Old Testament Scripture when He said, " Verily I say unto you, Till heaven and earth pass, one jot or one tittle shall in no wise pass from the law, till all be fulfilled " (Matt. v. 18).

One can imagine the errors that would have crept in had not the Scriptural writers been miraculously preserved from error. A stenographer in a certain merchant house was asked by her employer to write as follows:

" GENTLEMEN,

" We misunderstood your letter, and will now fulfil your order."

Imagine his surprise when the letter came for his signature with the word " not " instead of " now." Only one letter changed yet the meaning was exactly contrary to that intended.

Some people claim that only the concept, or thought, was inspired, and that the writers were left to clothe this in words of their own choosing, but the testimony of Scripture is exactly the reverse, since God always gave the words, but did not always make the meaning of these clear. Compare the words of Peter: " Of which salvation the prophets have enquired and searched diligently, who prophesied of the grace that should come unto you: searching what, or what manner of time the Spirit of Christ which was in them did signify, when it testified beforehand the sufferings of Christ . . . unto whom it was revealed that not unto themselves, but unto us they did minister " (I. Pet. i. 10-12). Daniel also said: " And I heard, but I understood not " (Dan. xii. 8.).

Again Balaam said unto Balak, " Have I now any power at all to say anything? The word that God putteth in my mouth, that shall I speak " (Num. xxii. 38). So it was also in the cases of the old prophet at Bethel (I. Kings xiii. 20, 21) and of Caiaphas (John xi. 50, 51); both were seized by inspiration and spoke that which was farthest from their own minds at the moment. Paul says: " All Scripture is given by inspiration of God " (II. Tim. iii. 16). Here the Greek word for Scripture is *graphe,* which means anything written. But writing is composed of words, and thus this very passage proves the inspiration of the very words of Scripture.

Canon Westcott says : " Words are as essential to intellectual processes as they are to mutual intercourse. . . . Thoughts are wedded to words as necessarily as soul to body, without it the mysteries unveiled before the eyes of the seer would be confused shadows: with it, they are made clear lessons for human life."

Dean Burgon says: " You cannot dissect inspiration into substance and form. As for thoughts being inspired apart from words . . . you might as well talk of a tune without notes, or a sum without figures. No such theory of inspiration is even intelligible."

The language in which the Old Testament was originally written was, of course, Hebrew with the exception of a few chapters in Daniel (chapters ii. 4—vii. 28), a verse in Jeremiah (x. 11), and a passage in Ezra (iv. 8—vi. 18) which were written in Chaldean

B

or Aramaic. No doubt the reason for this is that these passages contain a special message to Gentile nations and are therefore written in a language which they would understand.

Hebrew was not, of course, the original language spoken by the first inhabitants of the world. Before Babel everyone spoke the same tongue (Gen. xi. 1), while, at present there are considerably more than 2,000 different languages and principal dialects in use. The earliest language of the world of which we have any knowledge was Sumero-Akkadian. This was the language of Sumir (or Southern) and Akkad (or Northern) Babylonia, the land of Shinar (Gen. xi. 2), and was probably the language used before the flood. " Adam," " Eden," and " Sabbath " are all Akkadian words.

The earliest form of writing was pictorial, or ideographic; that is, pictures conveyed ideas. For example, a jackal represented cunning or craft; a man's arm with a stick represented strength; a woman playing a tambourine represented joy. This ideographic writing developed in Egypt to represent sounds. Thus—

A was represented by an Eagle.
B   ,,   ,,   ,, a Leg.
R or L   ,,   ,, a Lion.
H   ,,   ,,   ,, a House.

In Babylonia, from whence Abraham came, this pictorial language developed into the cuneiform or wedge-shaped writing which was a series of lines roughly depicting an outline of the object. Clay, being plentiful in this region, was used for writing material.

Abraham, living in Ur, a city of Sumir or southern Babylonia, spoke this Semitic-Babylonian language. But when he entered the land of Canaan he adopted the language of the inhabitants there, which was that which afterwards became known as Hebrew. An interesting illustration of this fact is seen in Gen. xxxi. 47: Laban, speaking Chaldean, called the heap of stones of witness " Jegar-sahadutha "; Jacob, speaking the language of Canaan, called it Galeed. Another interesting proof of this fact is that the only word in the Hebrew language for " west " is *yam,* which is really the word for " sea." Since the Mediterranean Sea lay to the west of Canaan, the same word did duty for both ideas.

With regard to the actual characters used in writing Hebrew Moses did not use the now familiar "square" letters. The earliest form of Hebrew writing was termed " round," and it is likely that the Hebrews adopted it from the Canaanites among whom they lived. It is similar to the Phoenician writing found on the stone monuments and coins of that people. The Babylonian Talmud states that Ezra changed the form of the letters used in the manuscripts of the Scriptures from this "round" writing to the "square" form now used. It is evident, however, that in the days of Christ this latter " square " writing was in use since He (in Matt. v. 18) assumes the smallness of the yod (Jot). In the " round " writing the yod is a large letter something like the English Z in shape, whereas in the " square " character it is only slightly larger than our English comma.

It will be interesting for a moment to enquire what medium was used by the writers of the Old Testament to preserve the words God gave them.

In Egypt, where Moses the writer of the first five books of the Bible received his education, most of their writing was done on papyrus. This was made from a reed which grew sometimes to twenty-five feet in height, and yielded material for making writing paper. In fact, our English word " paper " comes from the word " papyrus." The stem of this reed was triangular; strips were obtained from this and laid side by side, then over these was spread a coating of gum and other strips were then laid at right angles across the others; finally they were pressed together. Because of the rough grain of the finished papyrus, it was only possible to write on one side of the sheet, namely in the direction of the grain.

It is interesting to note in passing that the ark, made for Moses by his mother, was of bulrushes, which in this case were papyrus reeds as the Hebrew word shows.

Long rolls of this papyrus, some written centuries before the time of Moses, have been discovered in Egyptian tombs.

Although Moses would often have used papyrus during his life in Egypt, yet it is probable that both he, and the other Old Testament writers, used prepared goat-skins to record the Holy Writings. These skins were fastened together and then rolled about a round piece of wood, fashioned for that purpose. The finished roll was called a volume. This volume was read by unrolling one side and rolling up the other side until the desired place had been found. When Jesus went into the synagogue at Nazareth and opened the book it was a volume, or scroll, of this type and He would have had to unroll the scroll until He found the prophecy in Isaiah lxi.

The earliest known scroll of the Pentateuch now in existence is the Samaritan Pentateuch at Shechem. The portion of Palestine inhabited by the ten tribes was called Samaria, and when the King of Assyria took some of the inhabitants of the land captive, he colonised it with people from Babylon, Cush, Ava, etc., and this mixed multitude were known as Samaritans. In the time of Christ the Jews had no dealings with them.

Under the Roman Emperor Justinian the community of Samaritan Jews was almost exterminated, yet in the sixteenth century a remnant was discovered in the neighbourhood of their holy mount, Gerizim, who still possessed the Law in the Old Hebrew characters. This is known as the Samaritan Pentateuch, and it has been said that it is impossible to make it later than the first century A.D., but that it may have been written earlier, and some put its age as the second century B.C.

The pen used by the Egyptians was a reed, bruised at one end and frayed out so that it was really a brush. There are some in the British Museum showing the actual red and black ink on them as left there by the Egyptian scribe of the time of Moses! It is probable, as Moses was trained in all the knowledge of Egypt, that he used a pen like this to write the first five books of the Bible.

For ink, the Egyptians used charred animal bones, or for the more expensive inks, charred ivory, mixed with gum and water. The ancient scribe ground his own ink on stone slabs with a little muller, and he used a wooden palette with holes cut out to take the coloured inks very similar to a modern child's paint-box. Some have been found in the tombs with the dry paint still in them!

Not only did the Egyptians use papyrus for writing upon, but also broken fragments of pottery, boards plastered with lime and pieces of white limestone of a fine texture. The fact that stone was often used on which to inscribe drafts of legal documents, etc., helps to an understanding of Exodus xxxi. 18, and xxxiv. 1. It would be no new thing to Moses to see writing upon stone; what made them remarkable was that the tables of stone were written with the finger of God!

Before leaving the subject of Egyptian writing it would be interesting to tell how it became possible to read the story of the past which the Egyptians left inscribed upon the walls of their tombs. Until the discovery of the Rosetta stone by a French officer of Napoleon's army in 1798 the hieroglyphics of Egypt were unreadable for none knew their secret. This stone later passed into the hands of the British and it is now in the British Museum.

It was noticed that three different sorts of writing were inscribed upon the Rosetta stone. The lowest was recognised as being Greek and was soon translated. The uppermost was in the hieroglyphic writing, while the middle was in hieratic, which was a running script of the Egyptian language used for business, etc. They reserved the hieroglyphics however for sacred purposes. Somebody suggested that the three writings conveyed the same message, and having the key in the Greek, it was not long before the others were translated. As we shall see later, many of the Egyptian records bear remarkable testimony to the truth of the Scriptures, so it was surely in the divine will that these things should be discovered in order to close the mouth of the critic and infidel.

CHAPTER II

The Bible in Manuscript

A SHORT while ago it was the contention of the critic that the art of writing was not known in the days of Moses. Therefore it followed that he could not have been the writer of the Pentateuch. This in spite of the fact that the Scriptures continually declare that Moses did write these books and Christ added His testimony to the fact by saying, " He [Moses] wrote of Me " (John v. 46).

Recently, however, there have been discovered many ancient monuments that bear testimony to the fact that the art of writing was known a long time prior to the age of Moses. In the Tel-el-Amarna clay tablets, discovered in Egypt in 1887, we have proof of an extensive culture both in Palestine and in Egypt at a period before the time of Moses.

The story of their discovery is romantic. An Egyptian peasant woman was walking among the ruins of this ancient city, where sand had drifted on the fallen masonry which had once been the palace of a king. Little did she realise what lay beneath her feet. She was looking for something to sell, when suddenly her foot struck against something hard in the sand. Examining it closely she saw it was a piece of hardened clay, covered with queer marks which looked like writing. The tablet was shown to her friends and they dug for more, finding whole sackfuls of baked clay tablets. When the dealer in antiquities saw them, however, he shook his head and offered very little money for them. Yet all unknowingly this peasant woman had stumbled upon what remained of the Egyptian foreign office of the period,

11

and the clay tablets were letters sent to the Pharaoh from his officials in far-off Palestine.

Professor Sayce in *Higher Criticism and the Monuments* says: " . . . the letters are all written upon clay in the cuneiform characters of Babylonia. . . . They testify to an active and extensive correspondence, carried on, not by a select caste of scribes, but by every one who pretended to the rank and education of a gentleman . . . and the art of writing and reading must have been as widely spread as it was in Europe before the days of the penny post." Indeed, it is now definitely known that the art of writing goes back in the mists of antiquity, to the days before the Flood.

Commenced by Moses, one by one the writers of the Old Testament books added their part to the great whole, and without realising it, built up the great unity which we call the Bible. The wonderful organic oneness of the Scriptures is one of its internal proofs of divine inspiration. Written by about forty different authors over a period of about 1,600 years, each part nevertheless fits into the complete whole.

In order to grasp how really wonderful this unity is, let us suppose forty different people, without any pre-arrangement, enter one by one into a room, strike a few notes or chords upon a piano, and then pass out again. One would expect to hear startling discords, varying rhythm, and different keys. If, instead, we hear a masterpiece of harmony the only explanation possible would be that of inspiration. So with the Bible! Its writers were of varying tastes, ages, and social position and lived in different centuries. Yet there is a unity and harmony in the Scriptures which mark them as having a divine Author.

Following the return from captivity, Ezra, according to the tradition of the Jewish church, with the assistance of the members of the great synagogue, amongst whom were the prophets Haggai, Zechariah and Malachi, collected as many copies as possible of the sacred writings and from them set forth the canon of the Old Testament. The word " canon " is from the Greek *kanon,* a reed or rule, and therefore means, when applied to Scripture, that which is accepted as the rule of faith and practice.

In the Old Testament only those books which Christ and His apostles recognised as the written Word of God are regarded as canonical. On this point there is absolute certainty since Christ constantly referred to the Old Testament writings under the terms the Law, the Prophets, and the Psalms (Luke xxiv. 44). When He spoke of them collectively He called them the Scriptures (Matt. xxvi. 54).

Into these three groups the Jews divided their ancient Scriptures. Since the Jewish canon contained all those books and no others, which are now found included in our Old Testament, we have, therefore, the authority of Christ for it.

In the New Testament those books only which it can be proved were written by the apostles or received their sanction are recognised as of divine authority. Thus the all-important matter of the canon of Scripture was decided by the internal testimony and intrinsic value of the writings themselves, just as the true character of a tree is evidenced by the fruit it brings forth.

In making copies of the Hebrew manuscripts, the Jewish scribe exercised the greatest possible care " counting not only the words, but every letter, noting how many times each particular letter occurred and destroying at once the sheet on which a mistake was detected in their anxiety to avoid introduction of the least error into the sacred Scriptures, which they prized so highly and held in such reverent awe. Moreover, each new copy had to be made from an approved manuscript, written with a special kind of ink, upon sheets made from the skin of a " clean " animal. The writers also had to pronounce aloud each word before writing it and on no account was a single word to be written from memory. They were to reverently wipe their pen before writing the name of God in any form and to wash their whole body before writing " Jehovah " lest that holy name should be tainted even in the writing. The new copy was then carefully examined with the original almost immediately and it is said that if only one incorrect letter were discovered the whole copy was rejected."*

There is the record of the warning given by an old rabbi to his pupil in these words : " My son, take heed how thou doest thy work, for thy work is the work of heaven, lest thou drop or add a letter of the manuscript and so become a destroyer of the world." So by such careful, patient work has the older part of our Bible come down to us from the ages of the past. Although the original autograph manuscripts have all been lost, we can see in this the wise providence of God, for had any of the original manuscripts in the handwriting of Moses, David, Peter or Paul remained in existence they would have been superstitiously worshipped by many to-day.

Do I hear you question how it is that none of the original manuscripts are to be found? This is easily explained when it is realised that the ancient Jewish scribe always reverently destroyed, usually by burying in a grave, after it had been copied, the old manuscript worn either by use, or blurred with the kisses of its readers. " This is a living Book," they said, " it should look new. God's Word can never grow old."

There are, however, in existence many thousands of Hebrew and Greek manuscripts which have been copied from earlier ones by Jewish scribes and others from time to time. It is by comparing these manuscripts together that the original received text

---

* " The Scripture of Truth," by Sidney Collett.

has been arrived at, from which our English version is translated. The three best-known manuscripts of the Bible are the Codex Vaticanus, which is in the Vatican at Rome; the Codex Sinaiticus, which was purchased recently from the Russian Government and which is now in the British Museum; and the Codex Alexandrinus, which is also in the British Museum. This latter was presented to King Charles I. in 1628 and arrived just too late to be of assistance in the preparation of the Authorised Version of the English Bible. It was originally written for a Christian lady named Thekla, who was afterwards martyred.

It is an interesting story how the Sinaitic manuscript was discovered by Dr. Tischendorf in a monastery on Mount Sinai. One day, during a visit there, a monk brought into his cell some papers to make a fire. Tischendorf recognised some of the pieces as being parchments and looking at them closely, discovered they were part of an ancient copy of the Scriptures. His evident excitement showed the monks that they had an unknown treasure, and although he was told they had many more leaves, he could obtain no sight of them and had to leave the monastery with the few pages he already had.

Later he returned with authority from the Czar of Russia, the head of the Greek Church, to which these monks belonged, and upon his arrival was taken into a cell and shown the rest of the pages of the manuscript tied up in a red cloth. Later he left with these and presented them to the Czar.

The manuscripts mentioned here were written in Greek, but languages change and Latin eventually superseded Greek as the spoken language of the Roman world, and indeed remained for many years the diplomatic language of Europe. In the second century of the Christian era a Latin translation of the Scriptures was made and because it was in the common or vulgar tongue it became known as the " Vulgate." Probably it was this Latin translation which was England's first Bible.

In the fourth century, this Vulgate version was revised by Jerome who had access to ancient Hebrew manuscripts and so important was this revision that it has influenced all future translations.

Since the Scriptures were given to be a light to the world, and as few but the learned could read Latin, saintly men desired to translate them into the language of the people of England. About the latter part of the seventh century, Caedmon, an illiterate peasant of Northumbria, who worked as a farm-labourer in the employ of the bailiff of the Abbey of Whitby, sang to the music of his native harp the Bible story in the form of a poetic paraphrase. Bede, in his " Ecclesiastical History," gives the story of how Caedmon commenced his work. It had been his habit, when the harp came round to him and it was his turn to sing at the festive gatherings in the great mead-hall, to rise and leave the feast, probably because he knew not how to sing. One night he had thus left and had gone out to look after the horses and the cattle, when he fell asleep in the stable buildings, and as he slept he heard a voice saying, " Caedmon, sing to me." And he said, " I cannot sing, and for that reason I have come away from the feast." And again the voice was in his ears, " Caedmon, sing to me," and he answered, " What shall I sing?" " Sing to me the first beginning of created things."

So the words came unbidden to his lips, and in his dream he sang his song of praise to God the Creator. The sense of the opening lines of this hymn was as follows:

" Now must we praise the Maker of the Celestial Kingdom, the power and counsel of the Creator, the deeds of the Father of Glory, how He, since He is the Eternal God, was the beginning of all wonders, who first, Omnipotent Guardian of the human kind, made for the sons of men heaven for their roof, and then the earth.''

In the morning he told the bailiff, who brought him to the Lady-Abbess, and upon trial being made of him, he was found to have the divine gift. For no sooner had any portion of the Bible story been translated to him out of the Latin by the monks, than he forthwith sang it to the accompaniment of his harp in the short alliterative lines of Saxon verse. He was invited by the Abbess to join the company of the brethren, and became duly instructed in the entire course of sacred history.

'' And he turned into sweetest song,'' continues Bede, '' all that he could learn from hearing it, and he made his teachers his listeners. His song was of the creation of the world, of the birth of man, of the history of Genesis. He sang, too, the exodus of Israel from Egypt, and their entrance into the Promised Land, and many other of the narratives of Holy Scripture. Of the Incarnation also did he sing, and of the Passion; of the Resurrection and Ascension into heaven; of the coming of the Holy Spirit, and the teaching of the apostles . . . in all of which he tried to draw men from wicked ways to the love of well-doing.''*

Through this means the Scripture narratives were circulated for many generations in a form which fixed itself in the memory, and thus the common folk received a rudimentary Bible knowledge to which they they must have otherwise remained strangers.

While Caedmon was singing in the north, Aldhelm, Abbot of Malmesbury, who made a translation of the Psalms, utilised the same method in the south. He noticed how little the peasantry seemed to care for his English sermons, so one day he garbed himself as a minstrel, and took up his position on a bridge over which they had to pass, and having first en-

* Quoted from '' Our English Bible,'' by H. W. Hoare.

thralled his audience by the sweetness with which he sang, he tuned his song to a religious note, and so won over to a better life many whom a sermon would have sent to sleep.

The first real link, however, in the chain of translators of the Scriptures into English was Bede.   He lived in a monastery of Jarrow in Durham and was skilled in Greek and Hebrew.

Cuthbert, one of Bede's devoted followers, has told us the story of the completion of his master's labours, and a very touching story it is.   Through the whole of the eve of Ascension Day, 735 A.D., the grand old monk of Jarrow, the ablest scholar of his time in Europe, had been dictating, though with waning strength, his vernacular version of St. John. Evening came on, and then the night, but there still remained one chapter untranslated.   " Most dear master," they reminded him when morning broke, " there is one chapter yet to do."   " Take then your pen," he said, " and write quickly."

The spirit indeed was willing but the flesh was fast failing, and one by one the brethren came to his bedside to say their last farewells.   Then, as darkness again began to close in, the little scribe whose place it was to be near him bent down and whispered, " Master, even now there is one sentence more," and he answered him, " write on fast."   And the boy wrote on and cried, " see, dear master, it is finished now."

" Yes," murmured the dying saint, " you speak well, it is finished now.   Take therefore my head into your hands and lay me down opposite my holy place, where it was my wont to pray."

And so, on the pavement of his little cell, they laid him down.   Then saying " Glory be to the Father, to the Son, and to the Holy Ghost " his spirit fled.*

---

* Quoted from " Our English Bible."

Alfred the Great was also a translator of the Scriptures. Being aware of his own ignorance and seeing the darkness among his people, he drew around him capable teachers. One was Asser, the first scholar in Wales, who after some persuasion agreed to live at his court for six months each year. Alfred learned Latin from him by carrying in his bosom a little book in which every quotation of Scripture that pleased him was put down by his friend, Asser, and translated. The King was engaged upon a version of the Psalms at the time of his death.*

The honour of being the first to translate the complete Bible into English, however, belongs to John Wycliffe, the great reformer. He determined to prepare a great antidote to the " poison " of Rome in his complete translation of the Bible into the English tongue. At first under the powerful protection of John of Gaunt, he later lost this when the Lancastrian tried to persuade him to moderation. Forced to decide between principle and expediency, the reformer had no hesitation. " I am confident," he said, " that in the end the truth must prevail."

In A.D. 1229 the Roman Church had passed a statute which enacted that no layman should be allowed to have any book either of the Old Testament or of the New, especially in a translation, " unless perhaps the Psalter, a Breviary, or the Hours of the Virgin."

So that Wycliffe and his " poor preachers " whom he sent out to act as missioners to bring the Gospel home to the peasantry of England, were in definite danger. In fact, Wycliffe himself admits that he expected to be either burnt or else to be put out of the way by some other form of death.

Knighton writes bitterly of him: "This Master John Wycliffe translated into the Anglic, not angelic tongue, the Gospel. Whence it is made vulgar by him, and

---

* " The Book and Its Story," by L. N. R.

more open to the reading of lay men and women, than it usually is to the knowledge of lettered and intelligent clergy, and thus the pearl is cast abroad and trodden under feet of swine. The jewel of the Church is turned into the common sport of the people.''

This translation occupied him some years and was completed in 1382. A later revision, which is often wrongly quoted as the Wycliffe Bible, was made in 1388 by John Purvey.

While our present English Bible is different in literary form from this translation many of its phrases remain embedded in our Authorised Version. Such renderings as "compass sea and land," "first-fruits," " strait gate," " make whole," " savourest not the things of God," " enter thou into the joy of thy Lord," are as familiar to us as to those early readers of Wycliffe's translation.

Here is Wycliffe's translation of the Lord's Prayer (Matthew vi.):

" Oure fadir that art in heuenes, halwid be thi name, thi kingdom comme to, be thi wille done as in heuen so in erthe; gif to us this day oure breed ouer other substance; and forgeue to us oure dettis as we forgeue to oure dettours, and leede us not in to temptacioun but delyuere us fro yuel."

Shortly before he completed the translation of the Bible, there met at the monastery of the Blackfriars, in London, a number of priests, friars and monks to consider how they could best put down the opinions and teachings of Wycliffe and his helpers.

Just at that moment an earthquake shook London and some of the assembled doctors thought that perhaps their object might be displeasing to God; but the president, Archbishop Courtenay, declared it needed an earthquake of opinion and a violent struggle to be made by the Roman Church to remove such teachers as John Wycliffe, " whereat the meeting proceeded and condemned all his opinions. . . . "

Yet his doctrines spread so fast (the people being so hungry for the Word of God) that a writer of that day has angrily recorded that a man could not meet two people on the road, but that one of them was a disciple of John Wycliffe!

About the time he completed his translation he became ill and four friars and four aldermen, supposing him near death, came to ask him if he would recant his opinions. Wycliffe told his servants to raise him up in his bed and turning to the friars said, " I shall not die but live; and shall again declare the evil deeds of the friars!"

Although only in handwriting, very many copies of Wycliffe's translation were made and several exist to-day. Each copy took about ten months to write out and cost £40 in our money to buy. This was an enormous sum in those days and no working man, with his pay of three-halfpence a day, could afford it. Those who could not afford to buy a copy would pay a considerable sum to be allowed to read it one hour a day, and sometimes a load of hay was given for a few pages of the Scriptures. Detected copies, owing to the ecclesiastical hatred of the times, would be destroyed, and when we " bear in mind how difficult it must have been to escape detection, and how the multiplication of copies would necessarily be limited by the cost of parchment and by the expense of transcription, the survival for 500 years of as many as 170 manuscripts makes it clear that the Wycliffite translation must have been both widely distributed and carefully treasured."

Wycliffe lived four years after he completed the translation and died in 1384 of paralysis at Lutterworth. " Admirable," says Fuller in his quaint style, " admirable that a hare so often hunted with so many packs of dogs, should die at last quietly sitting in his form."* Four years after his death his grave was ran-

---

* Quoted from " Our English Bible."

sacked for his body, which was burnt and the ashes cast into the brook Swift, which runs near his Church at Lutterworth. The Swift conveyed them to the Avon, the Avon into the Severn and the Severn into the narrow seas, then into the ocean. Thus the ashes of Wycliffe were the emblem of the truths he proclaimed, gathered from the Scriptures, which are now dispersed over all the world.

CHAPTER III

The Printed Word

THE romantic story of the Bible would not be complete without a chapter on the printed Word. Nowadays a complete Bible, beautifully printed can be obtained for a shilling whereas before the art of printing was discovered a handwritten copy was very expensive and entirely out of the reach of most people.

The art of printing was invented by John Gutenburg, at Mayence on the Rhine, but the principles on which printing is founded were known to the ancient Assyrians, and among the ruins of Babylon have been discovered entire bricks stamped with symbolic figures and characters.

As Gutenburg was too poor to find the necessary money to commence printing, he had to confide his secret to a goldsmith named Faust. In 1450 the first book was printed; this was the Bible in Latin.

Faust undertook the sale of these Bibles in Paris. They were so beautifully printed that no one, except the printers, could tell how the work was done. As he offered his Bibles at 60 crowns, while the other scribes demanded 500, curiosity was aroused, especially when he produced copies as fast as they were wanted and even lowered his price. He was denounced as a magician. The peculiarly brilliant red ink which embellished his work was said to be his blood; and it was seriously asserted that he had sold himself to Satan. To save himself from death he was forced to reveal his secret.

The invention of printing gave a great impetus to the circulation of the Scriptures, and this aroused the

23

enmity of the Roman Church. A vicar of Croydon, in Surrey, in a sermon preached about this time, declared, " We must certainly root out printing or printing will root out us "; in which conclusion he was tolerably right.

The man who gave England her first printed New Testament in English was William Tyndale. From his youth he felt he had this one thing to do—to translate and print the Word of God in his native tongue.

He went to Oxford University and while studying the Greek New Testament by Erasmus he was converted. Feeling that he had in his hands the divine Truth he felt he could not keep the treasure to himself.

In the " Exhortation " with which Erasmus prefaced his New Testament he writes:

" I totally dissent from those who are unwilling that the sacred Scriptures, translated in the vulgar tongue, should be read by private individuals. I would wish even all women to read the Gospel, and the Epistles of St. Paul. I wish they were translated into all languages of the people. I wish that the husbandman might sing parts of them at his plough, and the weaver at his shuttle, and that the traveller might beguile with their narration the weariness of his way."

That which Erasmus only wished, Tyndale set out to do.

About the time when he was between the ages of thirty and forty, he was engaged as tutor and chaplain in the house of Sir John Walsh, a knight of Gloucestershire. Here he met many of the neighbouring priests, whom he exhorted to read the Scriptures. They answered, " Why even we don't understand God's Word, as you call it; and how should the vulgar understand it? It is a conjuring book wherein everybody finds what he wants." " Ah! " replied Tyndale, " you read it without Jesus Christ; that is why it is obscure to you."

One day a priest, angry with the strength of his arguments, said, " Well! we had better be without God's laws than the Pope's." Tyndale, fired with righteous indignation, answered, " I defy the Pope and all his laws; and if God give me life, ere many years the ploughboys shall know more of the Scriptures than you do."

Now that his full design had been divulged he had become a marked man, and fearing that his presence under the roof of Sir John Walsh might endanger his benefactor he threw up his position there and removed to London.

Feeling that if the New Testament were to be translated in England he must begin by obtaining episcopal sanction, he wrote to Bishop Tonstall of London to ask for his patronage. In due course Tyndale was summoned to interview the Bishop, but suffered bitter disappointment. " My lord answered me his house was full—he had more than he could well feed—and advised me to seek in London."

Fortunately, a rich London merchant named Humphrey Munmouth had heard him preach and befriended him, and for nearly a year he lived under his roof at Allhallows, Barking.

Then realising that no English printer would dare to print his translated Bible, and that he must either abandon altogether the great hope of his life, or else face the risks and hardships of exile, he took ship from London to Hamburg.

" I understood," he says, " that not only was there no room in my lord of London's palace to translate the New Testament, but also that there was no place to do it in all England."

In the spring of 1525, Tyndale moved to the city of Cologne where 3,000 copies were to be printed by Peter Quentel in a small quarto edition. The printing had gone as far perhaps as St. Mark when the work was suddenly interrupted, and Tyndale and his companion in exile, William Roye, had to pack up the completed sheets and make good a hasty retreat. A Roman Catholic named John Cochlæus overheard Tyndale's printers boasting over their wine that before long all England would become Lutheran. While they were under the influence of drink Cochlæus found out full details as to a certain New Testament which they were printing, and speedily laid information before the Senate of Cologne, who immediately took action.

In October, Tyndale and Roye arrived safely with the rescued sheets at Worms. Here they soon found a printer, P. Schœffer, who was willing to undertake the printing, and a new edition was prepared (with a view of out-manœuvring the enemy) not in quarto but in octavo. (It may be well to explain that the designations " folio," " quarto," etc., do not mark the size of a book; the size depends, in each case, on the size of the original sheets on which the book is printed. If the sheets are folded but once, the book is a folio, whatever its height and breadth may be. If folded twice it is a quarto; if four times, an octavo, and so on.)

These printed New Testaments were hidden away among bales of various merchandise and smuggled into England, in spite of the watchfulness of the ecclesiastical authorities, sometime during the spring of 1526.

Between 1525 and 1528 no less than six editions of Tyndale's New Testament (comprising probably about 18,000 copies) were published, yet so zealous were the spies of Rome that of all these only two copies and a fragment are now in existence.

" In burning the New Testament," Tyndale wrote in 1527, " they did none other thing than I looked for; no more shall they do if they burn me also, if it be God's will it shall so be."*

---

* Quoted from " Our English Bible."

It is related that the Bishop of London, having gained possession of one of the copies, entered into an agreement with a merchant named Packington to buy as many copies as he could get hold of, saying,

" Gentle Master Packington, do your diligence and get them and I will pay for them whatsoever they cost you; for the books are naughty, and I intend surely to destroy them all and to burn them at Paul's Cross."

Packington, being one of those men who love to conciliate all parties, ran off to Tyndale, with whom he was intimate, and said: " William, I know you are a poor man, and have a heap of New Testaments and books by you, for which you have beggared yourself, and I have now found a merchant who will buy them all, and with ready money, too."

" Who is the merchant?" said Tyndale.

" The Bishop of London."

" Tonstall? . . . If he buys my books it can only be to burn them."

" No doubt," answered Packington, " but what will he gain by it? The whole world will cry out against the priest who burns God's Word, and the eyes of many will be opened. Come, make up your mind, William; the bishop shall have the books, you the money, and I the thanks."

Tyndale resisted the proposal. Packington became more pressing: " The question comes to this," he said: " shall the bishop pay for the books or shall he not? for make up your mind . . . he will have them."

" I consent," said Tyndale at last; " I shall pay my debts, and bring out a new and more correct edition of the Testament." The bargain was made.*

" The Bishop," writes Hall, " thought he had God by the toe, when, indeed, as he after thought, he had the Devil by the fist."

---

* D'Aubigne's " History of the Reformation."

Tyndale did not rest content with what he had achieved and was soon busily engaged in translating the Old Testament. In 1530 there appeared a new volume containing a translation of the Pentateuch from the original Hebrew.

In 1534 he produced a revised edition both of the Pentateuch of 1530 and of the New Testament of 1525, and this latter has been taken to be its author's master-piece.

Tyndale was eventually captured through the treachery of a man he had befriended. This man decoyed him out of Antwerp, where he was then settled, acting as chaplain to the English merchants there. Outside the city he was kidnapped and im-prisoned. On 6th October, 1536, his enemies strangled him at the stake, and his body was con-sumed to ashes. Before he died, he cried out with a loud voice, " Lord, open the King of England's eyes ! "

During his imprisonment in Vilvorde Castle he wrote a letter to the Governor begging that he might be allowed some warmer clothing, and adding:

" I wish also for permission to have a candle in the evening, for it is weary work to sit alone in the dark. But above all things, I entreat and beseech your clemency to be urgent with the Pro-cureur, that he may kindly suffer me to have my Hebrew Bible, Grammar, and Dictionary, that I may spend my time with that study."*

Apparently his prayer was granted, for it is con-sidered certain that it is partly to his labours in this foreign dungeon that we owe the translation of that portion of the Old Testament (Joshua to II. Chronicles) which he left in the charge of his friend, John Rogers, who afterwards published the complete translation of the Bible. Tyndale is the true father of our present English Bible, and this notwithstanding the fact that

---

* Quoted from " Our English Bible."

it was Wycliffe and not he who originated the idea of a popular version. But the English of Wycliffe's time is not our English, and Wycliffe's Bible was only a translation of the Latin Bible, whereas Tyndale translated directly from the original languages, Hebrew and Greek. " For felicity of diction, and for dignity of rhythm, Tyndale never has been and never can be surpassed."

Indeed it has been estimated that the Authorised Version of the English Bible retains something like eighty per cent in the Old Testament, and ninety per cent in the New of Tyndale's work.

The opposition to the Bible in English arose chiefly because the priests and friars were afraid that if every man had a copy of the Scriptures for himself, the need for their preaching would pass away. Many objections were made to the circulation of the Scriptures in the common tongue. Friar Buckingham declared,

" If plain and unlearned people read the Bible they will confuse the spiritual meaning with the actual words !" He gave three illustrations. The ploughman would be afraid to plough if he read, ' No man, having put his hand to the plough and looking back, is fit for the kingdom of God ' (Luke ix. 62). While the bakers reading that " a little leaven leaveneth the whole lump ' (I. Cor. v. 6) would then put too little leaven in the bread, " to the detriment of the king's subjects." The command to pluck out the offending eye would result, so said the friar, in the people plucking out both eyes and so the " nation be filled with blind men !"

Shortly before Tyndale's martyrdom the whole Bible was for the first time printed in English by Miles Coverdale. Coverdale was a friend of Tyndale and he used his friend's translations so far as they went but completed the translation himself, using the Vulgate and Luther's German version as the basis for it.

This Bible bore the date October 4th, 1535, and contained a dedication to Henry VIII. which was added in the hope of winning a free circulation in England, and was signed by his " humble subjecte and dayle oratour, Myles Coverdale." This issue was never formally prohibited in England, and the second edition published by Nicolson, the famous Southwark publisher, in 1537, was announced as appearing " with the King's most gracious license."

It is strange that this privilege should have come from the hands of such an autocrat as Henry VIII., who in doctrine and ritual remained to the last a strong Catholic !

Coverdale's temperament was entirely different from Tyndale's. He was of a delicate and susceptible nature, with a feeling for rhythm and an instinct for whatever is tender and beautiful in language. He had not the scholarship of Tyndale. Knowing little of Hebrew he had used the Swiss-German (or Zürich) Bible, by Zwingli and Leo Juda for those parts of the Old Testament which Tyndale had left untranslated, namely the historical, poetical, and prophetical books. Yet he has left his mark upon our English Bible in some cadence here or a happy rendering there. The following passages are illustrative of the golden coinage from the Coverdale mint : —

" Seek the Lord while He may be found, call upon Him while He is nigh " (Isa. lv. 6).

" My flesh and my heart faileth, but God is the strength of my heart and my portion for ever " (Psa. lxxiii. 26).*

Two years later, in 1537, followed another translation, by John Rogers. This was issued by royal license of Henry VIII. and thus was the first really authorised version. Rogers called his version the " Matthew's Bible " with the view, no doubt, of escaping persecution and death. His *nom de plume,*

---

* Quoted from " Our English Bible."

however, did not avail him since he was later martyred in the reign of Mary.

Before the martyrdom of Tyndale he had appointed Rogers to be his literary executor, and had given into his keeping the unfinished manuscript of his translation of the Old Testament from the Book of Joshua to II. Chronicles.

Using this MS. and availing himself of Coverdale's translation for the rest of the Old Testament, Rogers brought out the " Matthew's Bible."

When the Bible reached England, Cranmer wrote to Thomas Cromwell, Lord Chancellor, asking him to persuade Henry to license its circulation, and within the short space of a week or ten days the Bible was authorised. Probably Cromwell seized the opportunity of getting its forerunner, the Coverdale Bible, in its second edition, licensed at the same time.

In 1538 Coverdale was requested by Cromwell to prepare a revised Bible which was to be based on the text of the " Matthew's " Bible, but omitting the ultra-Protestant marginal notes which were ecclesiastically offensive and might get its promoters into trouble with Henry who was not a person to be trifled with, and when aroused was very violent.

Accordingly, in the spring of 1538, Coverdale and others went over to Paris where the printing of what was afterwards known as the Great Bible commenced. Here the party worked under fear of the Inquisition. As a precautionary measure they availed themselves of the good offices of Bonner, then ambassador at Paris and Bishop-elect of Hereford. As Ambassador he had the privilege of travelling without having his luggage examined. A little before Christmas, Coverdale, in order to be on the safe side, packed off his finished sheets from Paris in the keeping of Bonner. Scarcely had he done so than an order of confiscation from the Inquisitor-General was made. However, the officer in charge of the prompt destruction of the printed leaves was probably bribed for " Four great dry vats " of printed matter were sold as waste paper to a haberdasher, and, having been re-sold by him to Cromwell's agents, were sent over to London, whither Coverdale had already fled. Later, Cromwell bought up the type and the presses from the French printer, Regnault, and had them shipped to England, and in April, 1539, the first edition of this Bible was ready for publication. It at once took rank as the "authorised version " of its time.

In September, 1538, Cromwell had prepared the way for the Great Bible by an injunction ordering all clergy to provide before a certain day " one boke of the whole Bible, in the largest volume, in Englyshe, sett up in summe convenyent place within the churche that ye have cure of, whereat your parishioners may most commodiously resort to the same and rede yt."

This injunction had all the authority of a royal proclamation, and thus within thirteen years of the burning of Tyndale's New Testaments at St. Paul's, the battle of the English Bible had been finally won. First forbidden; then silently tolerated; and next licensed, it was now commanded by the King's Highness to be set up for the benefit of each one of the 11,000 parishes in the land.''*

When King Henry VIII. saw it he said, " Let it go abroad among my people!" thus answering the prayer of dying Tyndale.

Everywhere this Bible, also called " The Chained Bible " owing to the fact that it was chained to the desks of the churches for safe keeping, was received and read with joy. The picture, however, has its reverse side. Henry had accompanied his concession with the condition that the new translation should be used " humbly and reverently," " not having thereof any open reasoning in your taverns or alehouses," but reading it " quietly and charitably every one of you to the edifying of himself, his wife and family.''*

---

* Quoted from " Our English Bible," by H. W. Hoare.

But the Reformation spirit was too strong for men with little mental balance, and often the preacher, as in Old St. Paul's, was completely drowned by a tumult of voices shouting verses of the Bible out aloud in various parts of the church, and occasionally adding to them improvised expositions.

So great was the chaos that Bishop Bonner was obliged to threaten the removal of the Bibles, of which he had purchased six copies, unless the rules were better observed.

One other incident deserves recording. The fourth edition of the Great Bible, issued in November, 1540, recites in its title that it had been " oversene and perused by the ryghte reverende fathers in God, Cuthbert, bisshop of Duresme, and Nicolar, bisshop of Rochester." This episcopal authorisation was by the King's command, but the interesting point is that this Cuthbert of Duresme was no other than Cuthbert Tonstall, who had refused hospitality to Tyndale, and who had subsequently burnt the book on which, under its changed garb, he now pronounced his official blessing!*

In a later edition of this version appeared a curious translation which has given it the name of " Bug Bible," because Psalm xci. 5 was rendered, " Thou shall not nede to be afrayed for eny bugges by night."† Compare, for the use of the word bug in this sense, our words bogy, bugaboo, bugbear.

Towards the end of Henry's reign there came a reaction from Protestantism to Catholicism. Cromwell fell from power, Henry cynically left him to his enemies and he was executed in July, 1540. With Cromwell fell his Protestant policy. Already the Protestants among his subjects had sorely vexed and irritated Henry by their disorderly use or abuse of the Great Bible, the sacred words of which as he

---

* Quoted from " Our English Bible," by H. W. Hoare.
† " The Scripture of Truth," by Sidney Collett.

bitterly complained, '' were disputed, rimed, sung, and jangled in every alehouse.''

In 1543 all Tyndale Bibles were prohibited, and it was ordered that the annotations and controversial matter in '' Matthew's '' Bible should be effaced and made illegible.   Later even Coverdale's Bible was prohibited, and in 1546, there was a perfect holocaust of English Bibles and Testaments.   The Great Bible alone was left to reign in solitary grandeur, while the use of it was by statute forbidden to the great bulk of the people, and was restricted to the upper classes. In 1547 the king died.   With all his faults, and he had many, Henry VIII. did much to prepare the way for the cause of the Bible in England.   Politically a Protestant, because he could not avoid it, he emancipated his country from the Roman jurisdiction, while at the same time he remained, religiously, a Catholic to the last.

Edward VI., the only surviving son of Henry VIII., came to the throne at the tender age of ten.   At his coronation, seeing the three swords of state being borne before him, he asked where was the fourth sword—the Sword of the Spirit?   They handed him a Bible and this incident made such an impression on the nation that since then the presentation of a Bible to the sovereign has formed a part of the English coronation ceremony.

During his reign measures were taken to establish Protestantism as the religion of the State; the church service was commanded to be read in English; the Communion cup was to be allowed to the laity; and the laws prohibiting the marriage of priests were declared void.   Unhappily Edward did not live long and he was succeeded by Queen Mary.   During her reign the circulation of the Bible was again forbidden, and many Bible-loving men and women were burned at the stake.   Among these were Ridley, Latimer and Cranmer.   Latimer was committed to the Tower shortly after the accession of

Mary and, steadfastly maintaining his faith, he was led to the stake with Ridley on 16th October, 1555. Before they lit the flame he turned to his companion, saying, " Be of good courage, Master Ridley, and play the man ; we shall this day light such a candle in England, as by God's grace shall never be put out." Gunpowder being fastened about his body to hasten his death, it took fire with the first flame, and he died immediately.

Cranmer had laboured incessantly to forward the reformation and when Mary became Queen, his friends advised his flight. He refused to do so, however, and was later committed to the Tower. Shortly before his execution, having until this moment maintained admirable constancy, he recanted. This recantation could not, however, preserve his life, and on the day of his execution he solemnly addressed the people, openly declaring his faith, saying, " Forasmuch as my hand offended in writing contrary to my heart, therefore my hand shall first be punished. For, if I may come to the fire, it shall be first burned. And as for the Pope, I refuse him, as Christ's enemy and anti-christ, with all his false doctrine." He was hurried away to the stake, where he stood motionless, holding up his right hand, and exclaiming, until his utterance was stifled, " This unworthy hand ! Lord Jesus, receive my spirit ! "

In 1560, two years after Queen Elizabeth came to the throne, the " Geneva Bible " appeared. It was thus called because it was prepared by the Reformers who fled to Geneva during the reign of Mary. It was distinguished for its learning and was translated directly from the original Hebrew and Greek. It was also the first Bible to divide the chapters into verses and to use italics to indicate words that were not in the original. It is also known as the " Breeches Bible " because Genesis iii. 7 is there translated, " They sewed fig leaves together and made themselves breeches."

This version had a wonderful success. Between 1560 and the Civil War, 160 editions of it passed into circulation, sixty of them during the reign of Elizabeth alone. In Scotland it speedily established itself as the household Bible.

There being very little secular literature at this time the habit of Bible reading steadily gained a firm hold upon the community.

The Genevan version, then, constitutes an important link in the chain of English versions, and left to itself, it was inevitable that it should, on its merits, dethrone the Great Bible. It was plainly impossible that the Puritan book with its annotations should be allowed to become the standard version of England, and so a revision committee was appointed, and in October, 1568, the version known as the Bishop's Bible was published, strongly supported by Convocation.

On the whole this revision was not successful. It was costly and cumbersome, and the revisers adhered too closely to the renderings of the Great Bible for it to satisfy scholars. After passing through nineteen editions it ceased to be printed. There is no copy bearing a later date than 1606.

Its main interest lies in the fact that it is in the direct descent of the King's Bible, our authorised version of to-day, of which we would now write.

It is strange that this great masterpiece of English literature should have its origin in something like an accident. In 1604 Conference met by command of James I., who had come to the throne upon the death of Elizabeth in 1603. The sole object of the meeting was to discuss a petition by the Puritan section of the national church, but their grievances dealt mostly with the Prayer Book, not the Bible. It became evident that James was not favourably disposed towards their claims, and it seemed almost an afterthought of Dr. Reynolds, President of Corpus College, Oxford, and spokesman of the Puritans, when he requested of the king a revision of the Bishop's Bible on the grounds that they could not subscribe to the Prayer Book, since it maintained a corrupted translation of the Scriptures.

Conference was dismissed, but Reynold's request had fallen on a willing ear and it laid hold of the King's imagination. By July, 1604, the scheme for the revision was fairly launched.

All possible care was taken to secure the services of the best men available, and Puritan Churchmen and Anglican Churchmen, linguists and theologians, laymen and divines, worked harmoniously side by side. Forty-seven scholars, divided into six classes, to each of which a certain part of the work was assigned, assisted in this translation. Each person in the class was to produce his own translation of the whole committed to them and these several translations were to be revised at a general meeting of the class. When the class had agreed upon their version, it was to be transmitted to each of the other classes, so that no part was to come out without the sanction of the whole body. In 1611, after five years of close study, the Authorised Version was published. It is interesting to note that marginal cross references, which are so helpful to a study of the Bible, were first adopted in this version.

This version gradually took the position to which it was entitled by its intrinsic merits and became the Bible of the people, a position which it still holds to-day, more than 300 years after its first publication.

The revisers were men of profound piety as we know from the Preface to the Authorised Version which appeared in the early editions.

" In what sort did they assemble? In the trust of their own knowledge, or of their sharpness of wit, or deepness of judgment? At no hand. They trusted in Him that hath the key of David, opening and no man shutting; they prayed to the Lord, O let Thy Scriptures be my pure delight; let me not be deceived in them, neither let me deceive by them.

In this confidence and with this devotion did they assemble together."*

They spared no effort to make their work as perfect as they could.

" Neither did we think (it) much to consult the translators or commentators, Chaldee, Hebrew, Syrian, Greek or Latin; no, nor the Spanish, French, Italian, or Dutch; neither did we disdain to revise that which we had done, and to bring back to the anvil that which we had hammered."

They used " the ordinary Bible read in the Church, commonly called the Bishop's Bible" . . . as the basis of their revision, but were commanded " these translations to be used when they agree better with the text than the Bishop's Bible: Tindale's, Matthew's, Coverdale's, Whitchurch's (a reprint of the Great Bible), Geneva."†

It is necessary to bear in mind that they were not appointed to translate anew but to revise.

" Truly we never thought to make a new translation, nor yet to make of a bad one a good one, but to make a good one better, or out of many good ones one principal good one."

" The translation of King James's time took an excellent way. That part of the Bible was given to him who was most excellent in such a tongue, and then they met together, and one read the translation, the rest holding in their hands some Bible, either of the learned tongues, or French, Spanish, Italian, etc.; if they found any fault, they spoke; if not, he read on."—(*Seldon's Table Talk*).

Grotius wrote of England in 1613: " Theology rules there." The whole nation had become the Land of the Book, and the change was due to the extraordinary moral effect produced upon it by the spreading of the Word of God in the language of the people.

---

* Quoted from " Our English Bible."
† Extract from the instructions given to each of the six classes of revisers.

It only remains to tell of the preparation of the Revised Version of the Bible which was published in 1885. Nearly one hundred learned men of different denominations took part in this, and for over ten years laboured at the revision. " The demand for this version was so great that no less than two million copies were ordered before it was published. One hundred pounds was offered in America for a single copy in advance; while every word from the beginning of Matthew to the end of Romans—118,000 words, was telegraphed from New York to Chicago, the longest telegraphic message ever sent."* Although in some ways an improvement on the Authorised Version, it has never supplanted it in the affections of the people.

---

* " The Scripture of Truth," by Sidney Collett.

CHAPTER IV

" THE STONES . . . CRY OUT "

PART I.—EDEN AND THE FALL

THE title of this chapter takes us back to that day when Jesus, riding upon an unbroken colt, entered Jerusalem in triumph. The enthusiastic crowds, dancing and singing before Him, strewed their garments and branches of trees in His path, making a royal carpet for His progress. This was the great moment, the climax in the growing fame of the Master. Humanly speaking, had He chosen to put Himself at the head of the multitude on that day they would have crowned Him King of the Jews and raised rebellion against the power of Rome. But His kingdom was not of this world! And from that moment the favour of the fickle crowd evaporated. The same people shortly after were crying, " Away with Him! Crucify Him! We will not have this man to reign over us! " Such is worldly fame!

On this day of the triumphal entry into Jerusalem, the Pharisees murmured at the expressions of devotion on the part of His disciples and demanded of Him that He should utter a word of rebuke. Jesus answered, " I tell you that if these should hold their peace, the stones would immediately cry out! "

In an age when materialism is becoming more and more critical of the claims which the Bible puts forward to be understood as the Word of God, there are being excavated stones, monuments of the past, each possessing a voice, the sound of which is being heard over all the earth. The purpose of the next few chapters is to tell the romantic story of the way in which these monuments are verifying the truth of the Bible.

Excavations are being carried out in Babylonia and Assyria as well as in Egypt and every time the spade of the archæologist goes down into the earth the Bible-lover has cause to rejoice. Professor Sayce says, " We are but just beginning to learn how ignorant we have been of the civilised past and how false our ideas have been in regard to it. . . . The period of scepticism is over, the period of reconstruction has begun. . . . "*

As the early chapters of Genesis tell of events in Babylonia we should expect to find illustrations of them in this locality, and this is exactly what we do find. Let us examine a few out of many of the records of the past.

The Babylonians had a legend of the Creation, according to Berossus who was a learned Babylonian priest and historian. It was as follows :

In the beginning there was neither world nor men, only the grim monsters of chaos. " Over all of them there reigned a woman named Omorka, . . . in Greek being interpreted Thalassa (sea). . . . But when the universe was in this condition there came Bel, who split the woman in the midst and made the half of her into earth and the other half into heaven, and did away with the creatures that were in her. . . . Now, Bel, whom they interpret as Zeus, cleft the darkness in the midst, divided earth and heaven from each other, and ordered the universe . . . and Bel, beholding a place unpeopled yet fruitful, commanded one of the gods to strike off his head, to knead earth with the blood streaming thence, and to fashion men and beasts that could endure the air. Bel also made the stars, the sun and moon and the five planets."†

---

* " Higher Criticism and the Verdict of the Monuments."
† " History and Monuments of Ur," by C. J. Gadd.

It will be noticed that while there are many similarities between this legend and the record in Genesis, yet the historical truth has been so overlaid by superstition as to be almost unrecognisable. However, these legends do bear record to the fact and bring their confirmatory evidence to the truth of the scriptural narrative.

Traditions of the Garden of Eden and the Tree of Life exist, too, in this region. Eden, as we learn from the cuneiform records, was the ancient name for the " field " or plain of Babylonia.

A fragment of an ancient Accado-Sumerian hymn has been found which tells us that the " garden stood hard by Eridu, the good city," as it was called by the Sumerians, and thus in the very region where the salt " river " of the Persian Gulf was divided into its four heads. The Accadians and the Sumerians were the ancient inhabitants of the plains of Babylonia and lived there before the Flood. The hymn begins as follows :—

> " In Eridu a palm-stalk grew overshadowing;
> In a holy place did it become green: . . ." *

This sacred tree was a tree of life and is represented time after time upon the monuments of Babylonia and Assyria, some of which may be seen in the British Museum. Very often it was watched by two guardian spirits, or " Kirubi " as they were called in Assyria (the cherubim), who stood or knelt on either side, with wings behind their shoulders, and heads sometimes of eagles and sometimes of men. An inscription left by Arioch, king of Ellasar (see Gen. xiv. 1), or to give him his native name, Eri-aku, king of Larsa, who lived in the time of Abraham, shows that an oracle existed under the branches of this tree even down to Abraham's day. It is as follows :—

" Eri-aku . . . the executor of the oracle of the holy tree of Eridu, the shepherd of Ur. . . . " *

---

*"Higher Criticism and the Monuments," by Rev. A. H. Sayce.

No doubt we may see in these records the traditional account of the cherubims, with flaming sword, guarding the Tree of Life (Gen. iii. 24).

But what about the fall of man from a position of innocence to that of sin? Much of modern teaching would have us believe that there has been a steady evolution of man from the lower species, and that far from there being a fall downward from perfection to imperfection, it was on the contrary a fall upward! To the believer, the Biblical statement: " In the beginning God created the heaven and the earth " (Gen. i. 1) is quite sufficient to account for all the various beauties of creation. It is easier to believe in a personal Creator than a Blind Chance, the god of the evolutionists, for the " missing links " in the Evolution theory are so many and the gaps so wide, that the theory demands greater faith on the part of its adherents than does the simple fact of a Creator-God.

Our purpose at present, however, is to discover if the monuments of the past can bring any corroborative evidence of the Fall. The " wicked serpent " or the " serpent of darkness " was mentioned in Sumerian texts, and a fragment forming part of the Third tablet of the Creation series has been found in Babylonia, a translation of which (by Mr. Boscawen) is as follows :

" In sin one with another in compact joins
    The Command was established in the garden of
      the god
    The Asnan-tree they ate, they broke in two,
    Its stalk they destroyed,
    The sweet juices which injure the body.
    Great is their sin, themselves they exalted."*

It will be noted that this passage is, in many respects, similar to the Biblical narrative of Genesis iii.

---

* " Higher Criticism and the Monuments," by Rev. A. H. Sayce.

In the British Museum there is also an archaic Babylonian seal. In the centre, this seal shows a tree with branches and fruit, while on either side are seated figures of a man and woman; behind the woman is a serpent, its head on a level with hers. " This scene has been identified by some as the Babylonian equivalent of the temptation of Eve recorded in the Book of Genesis."*

The Egyptians, too, knew of a serpent of evil and sometimes it is shown in their drawings chained; at other times it is represented as being attacked by the god Horus, who is seen spearing its head. As some of the titles given to Horus strikingly resemble those attributed to Christ, it would seem that we have here a corruption of the promise given to Eve in Genesis iii. 15:

" It shall bruise thy head, and thou shalt bruise His heel."

The Egyptians believed a magical virtue lay in their sacred writing and that the pictures of which it was mostly composed had the power of coming to life. For this reason, when the serpent of evil was pictured upon the coffins of their dead, they often cut off its head lest it should come to life and harm the body of the dead person!

Before leaving the subject, we would note the remarkable fact that Satan has, down the ages, persuaded fallen humanity to worship him under the same symbol in which he first tempted Eve. Even to-day the Yezidis, living on the shores of the Mediterranean, worship him under the form of a serpent; they believe he will be restored to power!

That Eve was spoken to by a serpent may seem to present a difficulty. We must, however, remember that the instinctive loathing which humanity feels toward the serpent species, as well as its own crawling position on the ground, are results of the curse upon

---

* " Guide to the Babylonian and Assyrian Antiquities," British Museum.

it, for God said, " Upon thy belly shalt thou go
. . . and I will put enmity between . . . thy seed
and her seed." Therefore in its original state it would
arouse in Eve no feeling of revulsion.

Secondly, the fact that some birds are able to
imitate the human voice is so well known that one
hardly need give an illustration. God reproved Balaam
through the mouth of the ass, and it is clear from
the promise made to the woman, that in this case
Satan spoke through the serpent. The promised Seed
was none other than Christ, who at Calvary was surely
bruised in His fight with Satan, but who put His heel
upon the Serpent's head and shouting triumphantly,
" It is finished," gained the victory in His fight for
the redemption of mankind from the power of sin
and Satan.

The following, related by Bingley the naturalist, is
interesting as an illustration of the ability of some
birds to imitate the human voice:

" A parrot which Colonel O'Kelly bought for a hundred guineas at Bristol, not only repeated a great
number of sentences, but answered many questions;
it was also able to whistle many tunes. It beat time
with all the appearance of science, and so accurate
was its judgment that if by chance it mistook a note
it would revert to the bar where the mistake was
made, correct itself, and still beating time, go through
the whole with wonderful exactness. . . . "*

---

* Quoted by Samuel Kinns, " Graven in the Rock."

CHAPTER V

" The Stones . . . Cry Out "

PART II.—THE FLOOD AND BABEL

WE come now to a consideration of the story of the Flood, and although the infidel and the freethinker have mocked at it, in a remarkable manner the records of the past are vouching for its truth. Again the stones are crying out!

Before giving the evidence of this it will be of interest if in imagination we visit the royal city of Ur of the Chaldees, the home of Abraham. Long before his time, however, the city was an important one and its ancient inhabitants, who lived there before the Flood, were called the Sumerians. Let us visit the excavations at Al'Ubaid, about four miles from Ur. Sir Leonard Woolley says:

" . . . We have dug out part of . . . a primitive settlement. . . . In the ruins we found quantities of the fine painted hand-made pottery . . . rougher household wares, used for cooking and storage, hoes and adzes of chipped and polished stone, saw-toothed flints. . . It was clear that these people cultivated the soil and reaped their harvest of grain; they kept domesticated cattle, sheep and goats; they fished in the marshes (for we found fish-hooks and model boats). . . . At a date which we cannot fix, people of a new race made their way into the valley, coming whence we do not know and settled down side by side with the old inhabitants. These were the Sumerians. . . . Many generations passed, the acropolis of Ur rose higher and higher into the air as the refuse of its houses was piled in its streets

or flung out over its walls and ' then came the
Flood.' . . . The Sumerian Annalists in their
sober table of the reigns of kings made mention
of it as an event which interrupted the course of
history. They vouchsafe us no details about it—
' then came the Flood, and after the Flood, kingship
again descended from heaven.' "*

Some years ago Sir Henry Layard, when excavating
on the site of Nineveh, discovered what had been the
library of the king. In what he calls the "Chamber
of Records" he found thousands of clay tablets.
Leading from this library was a corridor down to
the riverside and along this were discovered many
more tablets, apparently dropped there when the
librarians, upon the sacking of the city by the Babylonians, endeavoured to save the records. Among
these were the Deluge Tablets now in the British
Museum.

According to the story on the eleventh tablet of
the series, the gods determined to send a flood upon
the earth and Uta-napishtim (the Biblical Noah) was
warned by one of the gods of the calamity that was
impending and told to make a ship in which he and
his wife and household, the beasts of the field, the
animals, and his goods, might find refuge and thus
escape the watery doom. He made a ship of the
size directed and smeared the outside with bitumen
and the inside with pitch.

At the dawn of the day after his entrance into
the ship there arose on the horizon a black cloud,
thunder and wind followed, and a mighty tempest
with torrents of rain. All living things were destroyed. The tempest continued to rage for six days
and nights until even the mountains were covered.
On the seventh day the storm abated and the wind
and rain ceased, but outside the boat " all mankind
were turned to mud " and the corpses floated by.

---

* " Ur of the Chaldees," by C. Leonard Woolley.

The ship finally stranded on a mountain called Nisir. After seven days Uta-napishtim sent forth a dove, but as it could find no resting place it returned to the ship. Next he sent out a swallow but that, too, came back. Finally he sent out a raven which flew away and though it approached the ship it did not return to it. Those inside therefore gathered from this that the waters were abated and came forth from the ship.*

Notably, the Tablets imply a moral reason for the Flood in the following lines :

" Why didst thou not consider but causedst a flood?
Let the doer of sin bear his sin,
Let the doer of wickedness bear his wickedness.

May the just prince not be cut off, may the faithful not be [destroyed]."†

It will be noticed that there are some slight differences between the Babylonian account of the Flood and the Biblical one. These differences are accounted for by the fact that the Babylonian account would be based on tradition and thus slight inaccuracies would creep into the narrative. On the other hand in the Biblical account we have the inspired record which is thus the true one. These slight differences in detail, while the main story remains similar proves another point. Moses could not have written the Biblical account by simply editing the records of the past, otherwise there would not be such a divergence. He must therefore have received a direct inspiration from God when he penned these records. This inspiration preserved him from falling into the errors that these heathen records reveal. In our last chapter we read of the Babylonian account of the Creation. Had Moses, as the critics of inspiration suggest, simply drawn his information of the Creation from these heathenistic traditions, we should have had a Biblical

---

* " The Romance of Archæology," by W. H. Boulton.
† " Higher Criticism and the Monuments," by Rev. A. H. Sayce.

record which in the light of modern discoveries would have been foolish. This alone is sufficient to prove that Moses must have been inspired when he penned these pages.

Further evidence of the Flood has recently been discovered by Sir Leonard Woolley. While excavating at Ur they found, in the earth removed, the remains of household rubbish, grey ashes, half-burned wood and broken pieces of pottery and came to the conclusion that these marked a refuse heap of the inhabitants of the time. Sinking their shafts still lower the character of the soil suddenly changed. Again I will quote Sir Leonard Woolley's own words as he describes the evidence he found.

" Instead of the stratified pottery and rubbish, we were in perfectly clean clay, uniform throughout, the texture of which showed that it had been laid there by water. The workmen declared that we had come to the bottom of everything, to the river silt of which the original delta was formed and at first, looking at the sides of the shaft, I was disposed to agree with them, but then I saw that we were too high up. It was difficult to believe that the island on which the first settlement was built stood up so much above what must have been the level of the marsh, and after working out the measurements I sent the men back to work to deepen the hole. The clean clay continued without change . . . until it had attained a thickness of a little over eight feet. Then as suddenly as it had begun, it stopped and we were once more in layers of rubbish full of stone implements, flint cores from which the implements had been flaked off, and pottery. . . . The bed of water-laid clay . . . could only have been the result of a flood; no other agency could possibly account for it. . . . Eight feet of sediment imply a very great depth of water and the flood which deposited it must have been of a magnitude unparalleled in local history. That it was so is further proved by the fact

that the clay bank marks a definite break in the
continuity of the local culture; a whole civilisation
which existed before it is lacking above it, and seems
to have been submerged by the waters.''*

So once again the stones are crying out the truth
of the divine record.

After the Flood, we read in Genesis that men
journeyed from the East to the plain of Shinar where
they built the tower of Babel with the object of providing a refuge in the event of another flood. They
set to work to build, using bricks instead of stone
and '' slime [bitumen] had they for mortar.''

This Tower of Babel is no longer standing but the
ground plan has been excavated and this shows that
it was similar to, although larger than, the tower
(or ziggurat, as these towers were called) at Ur. As
this latter is still well preserved it will help us to
visualise the Tower of Babel. These towers were
built in stages, each smaller than the last, in the form
of a pyramid and a temple usually occupied the top
platform. The whole was a solid mass of brickwork,
the core being of sun-dried brick and the outside a
skin of baked brick set in bitumen. Stairways led
from stage to stage. Sometimes these stages were
coloured differently, the lower stages being black, the
uppermost red, while the shrine was covered with blue-
glazed tiles and the shrine roof was probably gilded.
These colours had their mystical significance and stood
for the various divisions of the universe, the dark
underworld, the habitable earth, the blue heavens and
the sun.

Speaking of the ziggurat at Ur, Sir Leonard Woolley
says : ''No one looking at the ziggurat can fail to notice
the tall narrow slits which at regular intervals and
in rows one above another pierce the brickwork of
the walls. . . . These are ' weeper-holes ' intended
to drain the interior, a necessary precaution, for

* '' Quoted by W. H. Boulton, '' The Romance of Archæology.''

with damp the mud brick would swell and make the outer walls bulge if it did not burst them altogether." The reason for them arose because the terraces of the tower were covered with soil in which trees were planted and when water was poured upon the roots of these the surplus drained away through the " weeper-holes."

Thus did these ancient people seek to make a mountain tower that would save them from another flood. Migrating from the mountainous country where the Ark first rested after the Flood, they sought to build an artificial mountain with trees to form a " high place " for their worship. In this connection it is interesting to note that the word " Babel " is the Assyrian *Babili* which means the " Gate of God," and coupled with the fact that the topmost stage was often coloured to represent the heavens would explain Genesis xi. 4: " And they said, Go to, let us build us a city and a tower, whose top may reach unto heaven; . . . "

Fragments of a Babylonian tablet have been discovered in which references are made to the Tower of Babel. In this we read of " the holy mound " and how the god " in anger destroyed the secret designs " of the builders and " made strange their counsel."[*] Another tablet translated by George Smith reveals that it was built in seven stages.

It is interesting to note that the Babylonians themselves believed the Tower of Babel to have been built by the gods.

The ruins of the Tower were still standing in the time of Nebuchadnezzar, King of Babylon, for there are records, now in the British Museum, of his repairing this and also a similar one at Borsippa, a town near Babylon but on the other side of the River Euphrates. This latter he rebuilt as a tower with seven stages and his own account is as follows: _

* " Higher Criticism and the Monuments," by Rev. A. H. Sayce.

" At that time Euriminaki, the Tower of Borsippa, which a former king had made . . . from distant days it had fallen into decay, and the outlets of its water were not kept in order. Rain and running had torn its brick-work ; the kiln-brick of its casing was broken away and the sun-dried brick of its mass was thrown up in heaps . . . the kiln-brick of its casing which had fallen I joined together, and the pieces of it I set up, and the writing of my name on the repairs of its fallen parts I placed. . . . "*

It is interesting that Nebuchadnezzar talks of writing his name on the repairs for it is found that about nine out of every ten bricks of the ruins of Babylon have his name upon them and thus again the accuracy of the Bible is demonstrated, for Nebuchadnezzar, according to Daniel iv. 30, walking one day on the terrace of his palace, said,

" Is not this great Babylon that I have built? . . ."

Yet once more the Tower of Babel appears in history. When Alexander the Great arrived in Babylon he found it in ruins, and gave orders to rebuild it; however, he who had conquered the world was himself conquered by death, and he did not live to carry out this work. So all that remains of this once proud tower is just the ground plan and mounds of earth to mark the site of bygone glories.

---

* Translation by Rev. C. J. Ball, quoted in " Graven in the Rock," by Samuel Kinns.

CHAPTER VI

" The Stones . . . Cry Out "

PART III.—ABRAHAM, HIS LIFE AND TIMES

THE subject of this chapter is Abraham, or Abram as he was at first called, and we shall find much, among the records of the past, that will throw light upon his life and times. Dominating the town of Ur, which was his early home, must have stood the ziggurat, of which we read in the last chapter, and Abraham must often have climbed its grand stairways and gazed from its topmost stage upon the cultivated and beautiful plain stretched out below him. The houses which he would see built around the tower base were not unlike any modern eastern house, and from recent excavations it has been shown that Ur was no mean city.

It will be interesting to listen again to Sir Leonard Woolley as he describes the houses of Abraham's day. He says :

" It was one of the oldest parts of the city, where for many hundreds of years houses had been built and fallen in decay, only to pile up a platform for fresh building, so that by 2000 B.C. it was a hill rising high above the plain. Now the slopes were cut into terraces and the houses of the time of Abraham stood on varying levels stepped down from the mound's summit to flat ground below. When they were destroyed, the uppermost might suffer severely, but those on the lower terraces were deeply buried by the rubbish fallen from above and many were so well preserved that it was easy to picture them as having been deserted but yesterday instead of thirty-eight centuries ago. . . . In Abraham's time

men lived in houses built with walls of burnt brick
below, rising in mud brick above, plaster and white-
wash hiding the change in material, two storeys high,
and containing as many as thirteen or fourteen rooms
round a central paved court which supplied light and
air to the house. The streets were narrow, winding
and unpaved, with on either side blank walls unbroken
by any windows, streets such as one sees in any
modern native town, impossible for wheeled traffic.
Against one house a mounting-block showed that
donkeys would be used for riding or for freight and
the corners of the narrow lanes were carefully rounded
off to prevent injury to goods or riders.

" Through the front door of a house one passed
into a tiny lobby with a drain in its floor where the
visitor might wash his hands or feet and from that
into the central court. On one side rose the brick
stairs leading to the upper floor and behind the stairs
was a lavatory with its terra-cotta drain; then came
the kitchen, distinguished by its fireplace and the stone
grinders left on the ground. . . . Though the walls
stood in some places as much as ten feet high, there
was no sign of ceiling-beams, so the ground floor
rooms must have been lofty, a great advantage in this
hot climate. . . . In the middle of each courtyard there
was a drain to carry off water. . . . Occasionally we
unearthed in the house ruins, some of the small clay
figures . . . representing gods and their worshippers.
. . . They have a further interest in that they are the
Teraphim, the household images which Rachel stole
from her father and Jacob buried under an oak in
Shechem.''* From this it will be seen that Abraham
must have lived quite comfortably while in Ur; he
was indeed a citizen of no mean city!

There is an interesting legend, given in the Talmud,
concerning the birth of Abraham. It is said that on
the night in which he was born, his father Terah was

* " Ur of the Chaldees," by C. L. Woolley.

entertaining certain counsellors and astrologers of the king Nimrod. As these were leaving his door they observed one star which swallowed up four others in each quarter of the heavens and from this they inferred that a child had that night been born who should rule over all the world. They resolved to counsel Nimrod that he should seek out the child, pay to its parents any recompense they asked and immediately slay it. Terah ridiculed this proposal, saying that it was like offering a mule a whole houseful of barley if it would first allow you to cut off its head. Hereupon the counsellors guessed his secret, and it was only by hiding the child and declaring that it was dead that Terah could save his son.

When Abraham grew up, so continues this legend, he became curious to know which was the supreme god of the many idols Terah had and when the largest was pointed out to him he wished to offer sacrifice to it. When the idol made no motion to consume the cake of finest flour which he had baked for it, Abraham was persuaded that these gods were false and in his father's absence he set fire to them. On Terah's return he angrily asked who had burned the images. Abraham said that the largest idol had burned the others but Terah replied this was impossible as an inanimate thing could not do this. So he discovered his own folly in worshipping false gods and was rebuked by his son. Whether these legends are true or not, they give us a sidelight on the days in which Abraham lived.

Later Terah, according to Josephus because he hated Chaldea after his son Haran had died there, together with his family left Ur for Haran which lay to the far north-west of Ur. Haran was like an outpost of the empire and its temple was dedicated to the same deity as was that of Ur, namely to Nannar, the Moon-god. Terah would therefore find himself more at home there than in any other city in the world. Josephus also states that Abraham had to leave Ur on account of the persecution which his reproof of its idolatry had aroused; from Acts vii. 3 we know, however, that God appeared to him while still in Ur and called him to leave that idolatrous city. After the death of his father Terah, Abraham received another call from God to go forth into the land of Canaan but even here he was not beyond the influence of Babylonia for in his day its rulers claimed also to be the rulers of Canaan (Gen. xiv. 4, 5). It was not therefore to a strange and unexplored country that Abraham had migrated; the land of his adoption would be full of Babylonian traders and probably officials as well, while from time to time he must have heard around him the language of his birthplace. Thus was he able to take part in the social life of Canaan, and indeed he was not unlike an Englishman of to-day who emigrates to a British colony, for in Canaan he was still in touch with the civilisation of Babylonia.

An interesting discovery of Mr. Pinches some few years ago was that of the name of Ab-ramu, or Abram, found in Babylonian contract-tablets of the age of Khammurabi (or Amraphel), king of Shinar (Gen. xiv. 1). The names of Ya'qub-ilu, or Jacob-el, and Yasup-ilu, or Joseph-el, have also been found, the " el " termination being the Hebrew for God. We can see, therefore, that the names of the Patriarchs were definitely in use amongst the population living in Babylonia in the time of Abraham.

But to return to the story of Abraham. In Genesis xiv. we read of the battle between the four Babylonian kings headed by Chedorlaomer, and the five Canaanitish kings under the leadership of the king of Sodom. The record infers that there had been a previous campaign in which the power of Elam was successful and for twelve years the conquered kings sent their yearly tribute; in the thirteenth they rebelled and in the fourteenth came the reckoning. Defeated by the Babylonian Confederacy, their cities were sacked, and Lot, Abraham's nephew, at that time resident in Sodom, was taken captive. Would that Lot had taken warning and, upon his deliverance later by Abraham, severed for ever his connection with that wicked city. He might have saved himself much heart-burning and loss!

It used to be the contention of the critic that the names of these kings were only Hebrew inventions and that it was impossible at this early date for the power of Mesopotamia to have been felt as far away as Canaan. Now, however, the critic is discreetly silent for there have been recovered fragments of old-world history in which the Biblical story has been verified even to the very names of the kings engaged in this battle. Indeed, Eri-aku of Larsa (or Arioch of Ellasar) gives his father, Kudur-Nankhundi, the title of " Father " or governor of the land of the Amorites, which was the Babylonian name for Canaan. Thus again the stones are crying out the truth of the divine record!

Hearing of his nephew's misfortune, Abraham hastened to his rescue and overtaking the enemy at night time, he was able to surprise them and to recover Lot and the other captives, together with their goods; on his return he was met by Melchisedec, king of Salem.

By the discovery of the Tel-el-Amarna tablets, much that throws light on this Old Testament character has been revealed. Several of the most interesting of these baked clay letters were written to Pharaoh Amenophis IV. by Ebed-Tob, King of Jerusalem. " Not only is the name of Uru-salim, or Jerusalem, the only one in use, the city itself is already one of the most important fortresses of Canaan. . . . Now Ebed-Tob declares time after time that he is not an Egyptian governor, but a tributary ally and vassal of the Pharaoh and that he had received his royal power, not by inheritance from his father and mother, but through the arm (or oracle) of the ' mighty

king.' As the ' mighty king ' is distinguished from
the ' great king ' of Egypt, we must see in him . . .
the most high God of Melchisedec. . . ''*

Ebed-Tob therefore owed his royal dignity to his
god and was indeed a priest as well as king.   His
throne had not descended to him by inheritance; so
far as his kingly office is concerned, he is, like Melchisedec, without father and without mother.   Further,
Uru-Salim means the " city of Salim," the God of
Peace, and there is no doubt that here was maintained
the knowledge and, in the midst of idolatry, the worship of the true God.   This will explain why Abraham
gave tithes to Melchisedec upon his return in peace
from an expedition in which he had overthrown the
invaders of Canaan.   Again, therefore, we see the
spade proving and illustrating passages that but
recently were held to be mere inventions concocted by
some Jewish scribe of a later period.

---

* " Patriarchal Palestine," by Rev. A. H. Sayce.

CHAPTER VII

" The Stones . . . Cry Out "

PART IV.—ABRAHAM AND HAGAR

SOME little time after the events recorded in the last chapter, Sarah, and no doubt Abraham too, becoming impatient for the fulfilment of God's promise concerning a son, adopted a human plan instead of awaiting God's time. How many of our sorrows are caused by our impatience and our unwillingness to await the due time of God's fulfilment. However, a point worthy of notice is that although Abraham had received the assurance of a son, he had not yet been told that Sarah was to be that son's mother and he may have thought that the plan proposed by Sarah was to be the fulfilment of the divine promise. It will help also to an explanation of Abraham's conduct in regard to Hagar if we examine for a moment some of the records of the past giving the ancient Sumerian marriage laws. The reader will remember that the Sumerians were the early inhabitants of the locality from which Abraham had migrated. In Sumer, monogamy was the law of the land but in the case of barrenness, so insistent were the demands of the East for sons to carry on the family name, concubinage was permitted. " The wedding ceremony seems to have consisted simply in the writing and sealing of the tablet—the marriage lines—wherein the position of the two parties was clearly defined. . . . " The wife had a measure of equality with her husband for she could keep and dispose of slaves and engage independently in business. However a barren wife could be divorced, taking back her dowry and receiving a sum of money by way of compensation, otherwise the husband could take a second wife. " A wife might present to her husband one of her own slaves as a concubine; on giving birth to a child the slave woman automatically became free but was by no means the equal of her old mistress; indeed should she rashly aim at becoming her rival, the mistress could reduce her again to slavery, and sell her or otherwise get rid of her from the house."*

The evil of this measure, however, soon appeared in its effects and Hagar, at the prospect of becoming a mother, became so exalted in her own sight that she no longer gave Sarah the respect due to her. Sarah, by that reaction which is often observed in human character, now began to regard with dislike the one who had been the instrument of her own designs and also, no doubt, remembering the Sumerian laws of which mention has been made above, determined to deal harshly with her rival.

Hagar fled from her mistress, intending probably to return to Egypt, but was met by the angel of the Lord who gave her the comforting assurance that she was not forsaken and that her son would be a wild man [Hebrew, ' a wild ass man ']; his hand would be against every man, and every man's hand would be against him : and he should dwell in the presence of all his brethren (Gen. xvi. 12).

Remarkably, for more than 3,000 years has this prophecy been fulfilled. Other nations have waxed and waned; have risen to world domination and in their turn been dominated. The empires of Assyria, Persia, Greece and Rome have all failed to conquer the Arab. None has driven him from his home or has been able to curb his free roving spirit; he has ever dwelt in the presence of all his brethren. Like the wild ass, the Arab has been untameable, his hand against every man. Even to-day, with Palestine again the national home for the Jews, the Arab still dwells

* "The Sumerians," by C. Leonard Woolley.

in the presence of his brethren and the descendants of Ishmael still prove a thorn in the side of the descendants of Isaac. How wonderfully has this prophecy been fulfilled and what a proof of the inspiration of the Scriptures !

Some fourteen years pass and one day as Abraham was sitting in his tent, the Lord, accompanied by two angels, appeared to him with the sorrowful tidings of judgment upon the wicked cities of the plain.

The story of Abraham's faithful intercession on behalf of these cities and of its failure because of their total depravity; of God's merciful warning to Lot and his family and of their escape; of the judgment by fire which befell Sodom and Gomorrah; all these are so well known that it is not necessary to enter into details. There are, however, two points that will be made clearer by a reference to discoveries made in the vicinity of the Dead Sea.

That the surrounding district was of a bituminous nature is proved by Genesis xiv. 10, where the Vale of Siddim, which lay probably to the north of Sodom, is said to have been full of slime pits. In fact the limestone hills of the neighbourhood are so saturated with bitumen as to have become perfectly black and to burn like coal. It is this stone which is used for black ornaments and sold in Palestine as Dead Sea stone. When polished it resembles black marble.

It is also known that there exist quantities of petroleum in this neighbourhood and from the narrative in Genesis xix. we see that the destruction was sudden and unexpected; that it was caused by "brimstone and fire "; that these were rained down from the sky; that a dense column of smoke ascended to a great height, like the smoke of a furnace and that along with, or immediately after, the fire there was an emission of brine or saline mud capable of encrusting bodies.

In this description we can see a bitumen or petroleum eruption similar to those which, on a smaller scale, have been so destructive in the oil regions of U.S.A. " They arise from the existence of reservoirs of compressed inflammable gas, along with petroleum and water, existing at considerable depths below the surface. When these are penetrated as by a well or borehole, the gas escapes with explosive force, carrying petroleum with it, and when both have been ignited, the petroleum rains down in burning showers and floats in flames over the ejected water, while a dense smoke towers high into the air and the inrushing draught may produce a vortex, carrying upward to a still greater height and distributing still more widely the burning material, which is almost inextinguishable and most destructive to life and to buildings.

" Indeed Sir J. W. Dawson, the famous geologist, tells how in a petroleum district of Canada a bore-hole struck a reservoir of compressed gas which, rushing upwards, spontaneously ignited, throwing up a dense smoke together with burning bitumen and wrapping fifteen acres of country in its resultant flame.

" The country around the Dead Sea has itself proved the best commentary upon the inspired text. Professor Emerson, one of our most eminent geologists, describes the region as one where sulphur, deposited by many hot springs, is abundant in the clay and where bitumen ("slime" or asphalt) oozes from every crevice of the rock and every earthquake dislodges great sheets of it from the bottom of the lake."*

Although, as we have seen, the natural condition of the plain of Sodom was such as to make its destruction by fire possible, yet we must not forget the providential character of this catastrophe. The " Lord rained upon Sodom and upon Gomorrah brimstone and fire from the Lord out of heaven " and thus did rebuke sin, providing a warning for all time that when

---

* " Confirming the Scriptures," by T. Miller Neatby.

destitute of " ten righteous men " judgment must come. The world little knows what it owes to the unknown and often despised followers of the Lord Jesus Christ. They are the salt of the earth, preserving it from corruption and many times the prayers of the godly have withheld from destruction some modern Sodom. When, upon the second advent of Christ, the believers are taken out of this world then swiftly will its final corruption be consummated and sudden destruction come upon them (I. Thess. v. 2, 3).

One further point needs explaining, namely, the tragedy of Lot's wife, who became a pillar of salt because she, in her regret for the loss of the pleasures of the life she had loved too well, hung back behind the rest and was overwhelmed by the storm.

One writer says, " It is curious how many difficulties are caused by the deliberate or unconscious neglect of that ordinary common sense in dealing with accounts in the Bible which we freely use in dealing with any other history. Thus supposing that we were to read that someone in the Alps was overtaken by a snowstorm, fell into a deadly stupor, and became a ' pillar of snow ' we should understand the writer to be using a picturesque expression to tell of a perfectly possible occurrence."

Lot's wife, as she stood staring about, was " suddenly wrapt in a sheet of nitro-sulphureous matter, which congealing into a crust as hard as stone, made her appear a pillar of salt, her body being, as it were, candied in it." Let us picture for a moment this terrific storm of lightning and tempest which burst upon the doomed district, the lightning igniting the bitumen pits, this followed by an eruption, which like a flow of lava, caught up and overwhelmed Lot's wife.

At the destruction of Pompeii in A.D. 79 by an eruption of Vesuvius many of the inhabitants were overwhelmed by the storm and were literally coated by the showers of fine ash and red-hot cinders, mingled with water, which fell upon the doomed town.

It has been possible to recover the exact form and features of those who died in this way. Thus a dog was discovered to have been straining at its leash, while seeking to escape from the overwhelming horror; a soldier died on guard at his post, refusing to run for safety; and an old man, apparently too ill to flee, died where he lay.

There is also an instance recorded by Aventinus who states that in his time " about fifty country people, with their cows and calves, were, in Carinthia, destroyed by the strong and suffocating saline exhalations which arose out of the earth immediately upon the earthquake of 1348. They were by this reduced to saline statues or pillars, like Lot's wife and the historian tells us that they had been seen by himself and the chancellor of Austria."*

The heroic faith of Abraham would itself make a fitting subject for a whole chapter but nowhere was his faith so tested as in the command to offer his son Isaac (Gen. xxii. 2). The enemies of the Bible have sought from this story to hold up the Scriptures to ridicule, claiming that it justifies the horrible practice of human sacrifice.

That there was a fierce ritual in ancient Babylonia which demanded human sacrifice we know from the records of the past and an ancient Babylonian text reads :

> " The offspring who raises his head among
>   mankind,
>   The offspring for his life he gave ;
>   The head of the offspring for the head of
>   the man he gave ;
>   The neck of the offspring for the neck of
>   the man he gave."

---

* Quoted by Kitto.

Coming from such a country, Abraham was to be taught a better way and the whole story, instead of teaching human sacrifice positively forbids it in these words, " Lay not thine hand upon the lad, neither do thou anything unto him " (Gen. xxii. 12).

Actually, God did not command Abraham to slay Isaac when He said " offer him for a burnt offering " as the original word used in the Hebrew is *alah* which literally means " to cause to go up." Thus all Abraham was commanded to do was to " cause Isaac to go up on to the altar for a burnt offering." There is another word which actually means " to slaughter " (Heb., *Zabach*) but the Lord did not use this word. Thus we see that Abraham was simply told to lay Isaac upon the altar as a whole offering to God. Whether God would require him to take the further step and slay his son, he did not know and would not know until the first command had been obeyed. That Abraham did exactly what God commanded him we know from the New Testament commentary upon the event, for we read " Abraham offered up Isaac " (Heb. xi. 17). When, however, Abraham took the knife to slay his son and thus went a step further than the original command necessitated, God sent an angel to stay his hand and by this divine lesson taught the founder of that race, which God intended to be the channel through which He would bless the whole human family, His abhorrence of human sacrifice.

Recent investigations at the site of the ancient city of Gezer prove that the early Canaanites were exceedingly cruel and explain why the Israelites were later commanded to drive them out of the land. Mr. Macalister, in the course of the excavations, uncovered a " high place " and found that the whole of the area of this high place was a cemetery of new-born infants, none of which was more than a week old. Some of the bones bore evident marks of fire and all were deposited in jars, the body being put in head first. This was no doubt an illustration of that horrible practice, so constantly denounced by the prophets of Israel, of passing children through the fire to Moloch or Baal.

CHAPTER VIII

" THE STONES CRY OUT "

PART V.—JOSEPH AND EGYPT

THE early chapters of Genesis have had, as we have seen, mostly a Babylonian background, but now with the story of Joseph we are brought into contact with another country and its customs. Palestine, lying as it did on the direct highway between Mesopotamia and Egypt, was alternately influenced by one or the other.

Some years have passed since the events recorded in our last chapter. The memorable visit of Abraham's servant to get a wife for Isaac, and later the flight of Jacob from Esau's wrath to his uncle Laban in Haran are all now matters of history. Jacob is home in Canaan again with his numerous family and his unwise partiality for his son Joseph.

It might be helpful if for a moment we digressed to ask the age-old question why God preferred Jacob to Esau. Humanly speaking, Esau is much more attractive with his bluff, hail-fellow-well-met manner, than is Jacob, the mean-spirited intriguer. In the scripture we read, " Jacob have I loved, Esau have I hated," and this statement has been taken by the sceptic to show the unfair partiality of God, while even the Christian, who has not carefully studied the lives and characters of these two men, is at a loss to explain the reason for God's choice. Much of the misunderstanding is caused by taking a passage in Malachi (i. 2) as if it occurred in the middle of the story of the two brothers in Genesis; but these words, as the context shows were spoken of the nations which had sprung from the two, according to the well-known usage by which the name of a great ancestor stands for all his descendants.

When the whole story is studied in Genesis, we learn under what conditions God's approval or disapproval were bestowed and we see that, as always, it is founded on character alone, while character, as always, is determined by the use or misuse of freewill. Jacob used his freewill amiss, it is true, and was punished for it. " Whatsoever a man soweth, that shall he also reap " is surely true. Jacob deceived his father and over-reached his brother at a bargain, but he in his turn was deceived by Laban and even by his own sons. Thus God marked His hatred of his sin. But although Jacob was mean and deceitful at the start, he was not wholly bad; "there was an angel in the marble," and God, like a great sculptor, with the tools of suffering and trial, set to work to get it out. Jacob, the supplanter, became changed to Israel, the prince who had power with God and prevailed, and became a standing proof of how a life can be changed when that life is yielded to God.

On the other hand Esau, with better chances than Jacob, with a birthright he should have prized, cared for none of these things. He was good-natured and generous enough at the start, and if he had cared to use the grace of God, which was as much within his reach as within Jacob's, he might have made a splendid character. Instead, he deliberately chose an animal life and, as always, the man who follows the blind instincts of his lower nature becomes at last a character hateful alike to God and man. Thus Esau becomes a warning " lest there be any fornicator, or profane person, as Esau, who for one morsel of meat sold his birthright " (Heb. xii. 16).

It is not, however, with Jacob but Jacob's son, Joseph, that this chapter would deal. It is difficult for a parent to avoid feeling some partiality for some one of the children, but a wise father will not allow this feeling to appear. Joseph, being the son of his first love, Rachel, was naturally dear to Jacob for his mother's sake and no doubt his personal character was such as also to endear him to his father. When, however, Joseph began to have dreams in which he figured as the hero, all the hidden jealousy of his half-brothers was aroused.

With us, in this present day, dreams are but little considered, while in Bible days they received much attention. There can be no question about the dreams of Scripture, they were certainly prefigurative and important. Has this door of communication with the invisible been closed or have dreams ceased to be significant? The prophecy of Joel, quoted by Peter on the day of Pentecost, was that " I will pour out of My Spirit upon all flesh, and your sons and your daughters shall prophesy and your young men shall see visions and your old men shall dream dreams " (Joel ii. 28; Acts ii. 17). Then Elihu, speaking as he claimed in God's stead, says (Job xxxiii. 14-17), "For God speaketh once, yea twice, yet man perceiveth it not. In a dream, in a vision of the night. . . . "

It is well known that dreams seldom arise during sound sleep, and in the simpler life of the ancients the sound sleep of physical tiredness would beget few dreams. Any that did come would be remembered. Whereas in our more complex existence of to-day the multitude of our interests, the high nervous tension of modern life, are all conducive to a multiplication of dreams which, being more numerous and less vivid, make less impression on the mind. " A dream cometh through the multitude of business " (Eccles. v. 3). Yet, even in modern times dreams have been given which have had an importance for warning, guidance, or for the detection of crime. Curiously enough a recent newspaper report gives the account of a dream which led to the detection of a crime. It

F

appears that a coloured servant of a Virginian woman hotel proprietor sat down on the porch of the hotel to await his mistress' return from a motor tour. While waiting he fell asleep and about four in the morning heard, in his dreams, his mistress screaming for help. Next day the man with whom she had gone returned without her and the coloured man's suspicions being aroused, he told the police. Later they found the woman's body; she had been murdered.

The enmity of Joseph's brothers having been aroused they soon took the opportunity of removing him out of their way. Sent by his father to visit them one day, they sold him to Ishmaelite merchants who sold him, in their turn, to Potiphar, an Egyptian officer who was captain of Pharaoh's guard. The Hebrew word implies that he was the chief of the slaughter-men or executioners. In the East, the bodyguard of the monarch usually carried out any sentence of death which he might pass upon any of his subjects.

What Joseph's duties were at first in Potiphar's house we are not told, but it was not long before Potiphar discovered that God's blessing was upon him and he advanced him to the position of overseer. The record says " he was a prosperous man " (Gen. xxxix. 2) or as one of the older versions puts it " The Lord was with Joseph, and he was a luckie felowe."

Some little time after this the wife of Potiphar, named in Eastern poems Zuleekah, tempted Joseph to sin, but he, strong in the might of Jehovah, resisted her enticements. Some few years ago there was discovered a papyrus roll containing the " Tale of the Two Brothers." This is now in the British Museum. In the first part of the story we have a faithful description of the life of the peasant farmer in Egypt. Anpu, the elder brother, lived with his wife on a small farm, and Batau, his younger brother, acted as his companion, steward and servant. The wife of Anpu conceived great affection for Batau. One day, when he returned to the farm on an errand,

she told him of her love; Batau rejected her over-
tures, left the house, and went about his ordinary
work in the fields. When Anpu returned to his house
in the evening his wife told him a similar lie to that
of Potiphar's wife and Anpu attempted to kill his
brother. He, however, escaped and afterwards became a prince. Although only a tale of fiction there
are some who think it may be based upon a traditional knowledge of the ordeal through which Joseph
passed unscathed, and of the ultimate position he attained several centuries before.

It is remarkable that, while Potiphar was chief of
the executioners, he did not cause Joseph to be put
to death. However, we learn from another papyrus
that Egyptian justice was very fair and even Pharaoh
himself did not summarily deal out death to those who
incurred his anger. The papyrus in question records
a state trial of great importance in the reign of Rameses
III., when men and women of all ranks of life were
implicated in a treasonable conspiracy against the king.
Instead of ordering them all to be put to death he
deputed the judges to find out the truth and to punish
the guilty, at the same time cautioning them to
beware of inflicting chastisement upon those who did
not deserve it. Thus we see again that the Biblical
record is true, even in the minor details, to the
customs of the country. It is upon internal evidence
of this nature that it can be proved that the writer
of Genesis must have known intimately Egyptian
customs. Genesis cannot therefore have been written
by some later scribe but must have been written by
Moses, who having been born and educated in Egypt,
would have knowledge of the smallest details of its
everyday life.

In reading the story of Joseph, we must remember,
too, the fact that the Pharaoh who reigned at that
time was one of the Hyksos, or Shepherd, kings.
These were a race of nomad invaders, of Semitic
stock, who conquered Egypt some time before the

entrance of Abraham into Canaan. Their weapons were the sword and bow, while the Egyptians at that time trusted in hand to hand fighting with battle-axe and dagger; consequently the Egyptians were easily outranged by the superior weapons of their enemies. This fact explains the rather obscure statement of the Egyptian historian, Manetho, who says, " there came, after a surprising manner, men of ignoble birth out of the eastern parts, and had boldness enough to make an expedition into our country, and with ease subdued it by force, yet without our hazarding a battle with them."

Later, when the sons of Jacob came to settle in Egypt they were given land in Goshen for "every shepherd is an abomination unto the Egyptians " (Gen. xlvi. 34). Naturally, the native-born Egyptian had little love for any who were of the same racial stock and profession as their conquerors.

Returning to the story of Joseph in prison, we are told that God's blessing was upon him so that he was soon freed from his fetters and raised to the position of assistant warder. One day he had two new prisoners, Pharaoh's chief butler and baker. The profession of these two court officers suggests that the offence of which they were suspected was an attempt to poison the king. Oriental imagination has supplied the details which the Scripture does not furnish and the Mohammedan account of this matter is that a foreign king, then at war with Egypt, sent an ambassador seemingly to effect a peace but really to find means of slaying Pharaoh. A woman of his own country, then residing in Egypt, advised him to get in touch with either the butler or the baker with the purpose of poisoning the king. This he did, but found the baker more tractable and by the means of a bribe persuaded him to his purpose. On his departure, he visited the woman but as he could not see her alone, he merely said he had reason to be gratified with his success. These words soon

reached the ears of Pharaoh, and as the negotiation
for peace had come to nothing, a secret of some kind
was suspected. The woman was arrested and tortured until she told all she knew, but as she could not
state which of the two palace officers was guilty, the
chief butler and chief baker were both thrown into
prison until it could be discovered who had consented
to the crime.*

One night, these two officers both dreamed and
Joseph interpreted the dreams. Three days later, in
accordance with the interpretation, the chief butler
was restored to his old position while the chief baker
was hanged. The severity of this punishment, when
it is remembered that the Egyptians were by no means
given to inflict the sentence of death hastily or for
light offences, seems to infer that the baker's crime
was a serious one.

Although Joseph entreated the chief butler to
remember him he did not do so and for some two
years longer Joseph had to remain in prison. One
night Pharaoh himself dreamed and the next day
Joseph was hastily fetched from prison to interpret
it. Once again we have an interesting sidelight on
Egyptian customs, for although the command was so
urgent yet Joseph stayed to shave himself (Genesis
xli. 14).

In Egypt, contrary to other Eastern countries,
shaving of the beard was practised by all from
Pharaoh down to the meanest slave. The only one
allowed to appear in public wearing a beard was the
king and even his was an artificial and conventional
one, which was strapped on to his face. In the
Egyptian gallery at the British Museum this beard
and its band can be seen on the sculptured heads of
Rameses II. and others. To the Israelites, on the
other hand, the shaving of the beard was a sign of
ignominy as we learn from the occasion when David's

---

* Quoted by Kitto.

ambassadors returned with shaven beard from the court of the king of Ammon. They were so ashamed that David said to them, " Tarry at Jericho until your beards be grown " (II. Sam. x. 5). Thus again we see the truthfulness of the divine record, for had Genesis been written by a scribe of a later day, as is claimed by the critics, he would scarcely have made Joseph perform an operation which to the Jewish mind was an ignominious one.

We have only space, in closing this chapter, to draw attention to a striking confirmation of the seven years of famine which God foretold in the dreams of Pharaoh. The Nile is one of the longest rivers in the world ; without the Nile and its annual overflow Egypt would be a desert. Its waters inundate the low plains along its banks, irrigating the soil and leaving a rich deposit of alluvium. Should it fail to rise sufficiently to overflow its banks a failure of the whole crop of Egypt would result and such failures do occasionally occur. There is historical evidence of a famine in A.D. 1064 which lasted seven years in consequence of too low a Nile, and the Arabic historian paints in terrible colours its results. The people of Cairo even killed and ate each other and human flesh was sold in the public markets !

At El-Kab, the residence of those native Pharaohs of the seventeenth dynasty, whose revolt against the Hyksos kings at length restored Egypt to its independence and raised up the " new king who knew not Joseph," there is the tomb of a certain Baba, who must have lived when the struggle with the foreigner was still going on. On the wall of the tomb is an inscription in which the good deeds of its owner are recorded with naive simplicity. Among other acts of charity which Baba performed, he states that " when a famine arose, lasting many years, I issued corn to the city each year of the famine." The evidence points to the fact that Baba lived towards the end of the reign of the Hyksos kings, that is to say the period in which Joseph was in Egypt and possibly this inscription refers to the famine of his time.

To write fully and completely of all the recent archæological discoveries that so wonderfully confirm the Scriptures would need a book in itself, and therefore we must, since the purpose of this book is more general, conclude this section of our subject. Enough has been said, I trust, to whet the appetite of the serious student of the Bible for further study of this romantic phase of Bible evidence.

CHAPTER IX

Eastern Customs of the Bible

PART I.—AGRICULTURAL LIFE

TO understand the Scriptures fully a knowledge of the customs of the peoples of Bible lands is necessary and it will be our endeavour to give a glimpse of these in the next few chapters.

We often speak of the " Unchanging East." Not only is change of any kind thought to be inexpedient, it is morally wrong—custom must be adhered to and no new fashions change the dress, methods or homes of the East. This being so, the days of the Hebrew patriarchs have been preserved as it were in amber and we can still study conditions similar in every respect as they were then.

There are three distinctive conditions of Eastern life in Palestine; the bedouin, the fellahin and the belladin and most of the Bible characters belonged to one or the other of these classes.

The bedouin are the desert dwellers. They are the sheep masters and herdsmen and they live in low gipsy-like tents of goats' or camels' hair sack-cloth, called " houses of hair." Abraham and the other patriarchs belonged to the bedouin.

Called to a migratory condition of life Abraham, while in Canaan, dwelled in a tent (Gen. xiii. 18) and it will prove helpful if we glance for a moment at these Eastern " houses of hair." At first it is probable that tents were made from the skins of animals, and a trace of this earlier custom is seen in the covering of the Tabernacle in the wilderness with rams' skins dyed red. Later, however,

76

tents were made out of a strong coarse sack-cloth
of woven goats' hair, naturally black or of camels'
hair dyed all black or striped. We remember that
the Bride, in the Song of Solomon, says that she is
" black, but comely . . . as the tents of Kedar "
(chap. i. 5). This tent cloth is quite waterproof and
possesses the property of absorbing the sun's rays
to a remarkable extent. However, the patriarchs
chose, where possible, the shade of the trees and we
know that Abraham pitched his tent under the tree
at Mamre (Gen. xviii. 4). In shape, these tents were
mostly oblong, supported by a number of poles or
" pillars " and divided into two compartments. The
smaller of these was closely curtained off all round
and was reserved for the women members of the
family ; the main part, or men's section, was always
open down one side and was used for the reception
of visitors. It was usually furnished, amongst the
well-to-do, with carpets, cushions and the camels'
huge and heavily upholstered pack saddles, lying on
the ground doing service as seats. It was upon one
of these that Rachel naturally sat, when seeking to
hide the household gods she had stolen from her
father (Gen. xxxi. 34).

In their private, curtained part of the tent, the
women would be able to hear what was spoken in the
reception " room," or men's part, and often by peep-
ing over the dividing curtain they would be able to get
a view of the visitor. Thus Sarah, although unseen
herself, would be able to hear the announcement that
she would, in course of time, have a son (Gen. xviii.
9, 10).

In the setting up of these " houses of hair," cords
or ropes were used which were attached to the
edge of the hair-cloth ; these cords were then looped
over a tent peg which was driven into the ground. The
larger the tent so the longer the cords and the
stronger the pegs required to keep it in position.
Thus God invites His people to enlarge the place of

their tent and lengthen the cords thereof for His blessing should surely increase, and they would thus need a larger house to contain it all! (Isa. liv. 2). To give a very beautiful picture of the security of those who trust in Christ, He is likened to a nail (or tent peg) fastened in a sure place (Isa. xxii. 23). If the reader has ever pitched a tent he will realise the necessity for a " sure place " for the peg; otherwise the wind will blow the tent down. Thank God, the tabernacle of life, upheld by Him, can withstand all the stormy blasts however they may blow!

As already said, the Eastern tent was divided into two sections—the completely curtained part being for the use of the women of the family. Into this part no strange man was admitted, and should one enter, the insult was immediately avenged by either the husband, or other near relative, slaying the intruder. In the much misunderstood story of Jael and Sisera we see an illustration of this unwritten law.

Among the nomad tribes of Palestine the rites of hospitality are held peculiarly sacred and inviolable. Base would that wretch be accounted who, having entertained a stranger in a tent, afterwards took his life while sleeping. In the story given us in Judges iv. 17-22, however, we see Sisera fleeing from Barak and seeking a place of concealment. In his flight he came upon the tent of Heber and as the men's section of the tent was open and exposed to the view of all who passed by, this would be useless for his purpose. Only in the women's private apartment would he find security and accordingly it was here that he hid himself. Instances have occurred and are recorded amongst the Arab bedouin of a defeated warrior hiding himself in the woman's apartment, but such a breach of Eastern etiquette has always been followed by sentence of death. Thus the insult offered to Jael, from the point of view of a bedouin woman, was such that to avenge her honour either her husband or brother would have been bound to take

Sisera's life. As it was she simply acted as executioner and thus herself became the avenger.

The fellahin are the farmers and farm-labourers and they live in the unwalled villages. They have always composed the bulk of the population in all oriental lands and formed the " great crowd " which followed Christ and heard Him gladly. It must be remembered that the Lord Jesus was unquestionably one of the fellahin since He was brought up in the village of Nazareth where He lived in the home of Joseph, the village carpenter.

The third condition of Eastern life was that of the belladin or townsmen. They were the merchants, shopkeepers, scribes and the governing officials. Their dress was more elaborate and their life more luxurious than was that of the fellahin.

The fields of the fellahin are not separated, as in this country, by hedges or fences but surround the villages in one unbroken stretch of arable land. When Joshua assigned the lands to Israel by lot, they were given not to individuals but to families or clans who held it in common and at sowing time these open common-lands were assigned afresh each year by lot among the villagers who possessed oxen with which to plough.

The method adopted was as follows. First the available land was divided equally into as many sections as there were farmers desiring to plough. An ox-goad or sometimes a measuring-line of twisted goats'-hair was used to calculate this division of the land, and a deep furrow or a heap of stones served as a land-mark of its extent. Each of the farmers then put into a bag or "scrip" an object such as a stone or small knob of wood and the presiding officer, usually the scribe of the village, called out the name of the section of land, asking to whom it should belong. A tiny boy, chosen that there should be no possibility of favouritism for, of course, not all the land was equally as good or productive, then placed his hand in the bag, withdrawing one of the objects; the farmer to whom this belonged cultivated that section of the land for the year.

This custom throws light upon those words of David : " Thou maintainest [lit., art taking hold of] my lot. The [measuring] lines are fallen unto me in pleasant places " (Psalm xvi. 5, 6).

We, like David, can rejoice that we are apportioned that part of God's great field, the world, where we have the blessings of His salvation. Had we been born into a family in some heathen land we should perhaps never have heard of God's love in Christ !

The land divided, ploughing began. As soon as the early rains fell, softening the hardened clods of earth, the ploughman had to begin his task. Sometimes he would have to plough in the face of rain, hail and even snow and if it be remembered that the fellah, when working, was clad only in his cotton under-garment it will be seen that he had no pleasant task. However, he must sow and plough with the early rains if he would reap with the latter rains for " He that observeth the wind shall not sow, and he that regardeth the clouds shall not reap" (Eccles. xi. 4).

Observant readers will have noticed that, contrary to western methods, sowing is put before ploughing. The sower, broadcasting the seed, preceded the ploughman and as he did so some naturally would fall by the wayside or path through the field and some would fall on the stony ground, for boulders are purposely left in the fields to afford the shade and retain the moisture required by the crops. Following him came the ploughman, ploughing in the seed.

Again it must be remembered that the Eastern plough is not of iron like our western ones but is a rudely constructed affair of wood having only one handle and a ploughshare which is simply a sharpened point of wood. Consequently the plough does little more than scratch the surface of the ground but as the soil of Palestine is naturally very productive this is quite sufficient.

With one hand on the plough and the other grasping the goad, a long rod with a sharpened point at one end and a small iron tool for cleaning the plough at the other, the fellah guides his plough across the field. To look back would be unwise for the plough is so light that should it hit a stone or a root it would be thrown out of the furrow and the handle would probably give the ploughman an unpleasant blow.

Hence the accuracy and point of Christ's words: " No man, having put his hand [not hands] to the plough, and looking back, is fit for the kingdom of God " (Luke ix. 62).

The plough was usually drawn by two oxen, but sometimes by asses or camels and a poor man who could not provide two animals of the same kind would be tempted to plough with one of each. This, however, caused unnecessary suffering to the animals, especially when a tall and a short animal were yoked together since then the yoke galled both. God expressly forbade the Israelites to plough with an ox and an ass together for one was ceremonially a clean and the other an unclean animal; so we are forbidden to be " unequally yoked together with unbelievers " (Deut. xxii. 10; II. Cor. vi. 14). How can we pull together in life if one is saved and the other not? The yoke will in time become galling to both !

The goad was used to encourage the animals to further efforts but an untrained ox would be inclined to kick against it. To do so only hurt the more. So Christ, when He gently reproved Saul of Tarsus while he lay on the Damascus road, likens his fierce opposition to Christianity to a wild, untrained ox madly kicking against the goad. " It is hard for thee to kick against the goads." (Acts ix. 5). From this passage one gathers that Saul had already felt convicted of the truthfulness of Christianity. Perhaps that day he minded the garments of those who stoned

Stephen and saw that martyr's triumphant death was the day that the shaft of conviction struck his soul. After this illuminating moment, excessive hatred of the Christians was the selfish reaction of his mad desire to drown all memory of that flashing insight into Truth. Human nature is like that! How many a man tries to drown his conviction of inner failure in drink! But every kick only drove the goad point deeper into the soul until Saul at last met his match on the road to Damascus.

The yoke was a piece of wood which was laid across the necks of the oxen. Its weight made the animals stoop. When God recalled to the Israelites their deliverance out of Egypt He says: " I have broken the bands of your yoke and made you go upright " (Lev. xxvi. 13).

What a blessed picture, too, of the man formerly bowed down by the yoke of sin but now freed to walk victoriously upright in the paths of righteousness! Some yokes fit better than others and therefore would be more easy for the animals drawing the plough. The yoke that Christ gives is an easy one and we are invited to take His yoke upon us and pull in the team that is seeking to turn the barren places of men's hearts into plenteous fields bearing the fruits of the Spirit (Matt. xi. 30).

Most of the fellahin are very poor so that at the best of times they live from hand to mouth. Consequently in seasons of great scarcity they part in sorrow with every measure of seed they sow. To them it seems like taking the bread out of the mouths of their starving children, especially as a dry summer may mean little reaping. It is with this in mind that the Psalmist graphically says: " He that goeth forth and weepeth, bearing precious seed, shall doubtless come again with rejoicing, bringing his sheaves with him " (Psalm cxxvi. 6).

The Christian, too, has precious seed to sow, the Word of God and the glad news of His love. But soul travail is necessary before the sheaves of this harvest can be garnered and if we would reap we must water the seed with our tears. Dr. Torrey tells of a Colonel Clarke who had a mission for " down and outs " in Chicago. Drunkards, thieves, pickpockets, gamblers and everything that was helpless used to gather night after night to hear Colonel Clarke talk in his prosy way and would listen to him spellbound, being converted by the score. The secret was that they knew he loved them and nothing conquers like love. Once in the early days of the mission, when he had been weeping a great deal over these men, he got ashamed of his tears. He steeled his heart and tried to stop his crying, and succeeded; but he lost his power! Seeing that his power was gone, he went to God and prayed, " O God, give me back my tears," and God gave him back his tears and gave him won- derful power over those men.

After the grain has been harvested it is threshed. A heavy wooden sledge is made and on the under- neath side are fixed sharp pieces of flint and metal. The wheat or barley is then spread out in a prepared place on the ground and the oxen are driven over the threshing-floor, dragging after them the heavy thresh- ing instrument which not only extracts the grain from the ear but chops up the straw. It was this threshing instrument which Ornan offered to David as fuel for the sacrifice of the very oxen that were dragging it on that occasion when David proposed to erect an altar in thankfulness for the end of the plague (I. Chron. xxi. 23).

The threshing completed, there followed the win- nowing. The heap of chaff and grain was attacked by the fellah with the fan. This was a wooden instru- ment like a many-pronged fork and it is to this that John the Baptist refers when he says of Christ that His " fan is in His hand, and He will throughly purge His floor, and gather His wheat into the

garner; but He will burn up the chaff with unquench-
able fire " (Matt. iii. 12).

The mingled grain and chaff was flung into the air
by this fan and the wind carried the chaff and crushed
straw away while the grain, being heavier, fell in
a heap by itself close to the winnower. The crushed
straw fell a little farther away while the chaff, being
the lightest of all, fell in a small heap by itself farther
out still. If the wind were too strong the latter
would be quite blown away and lost. It was, no
doubt, to this that the passage in Isaiah (xli. 15, 16)
refers when God says : " I will make thee a new
sharp threshing instrument having teeth; thou shalt
thresh the mountains and beat them small, and shalt
make the hills as chaff. Thou shalt fan them, and the
wind shall carry them away."

The comparison of mountains to the huge heap of
straw and the hills to the smaller heap of chaff is a
striking figure. How often our troubles, which seem
mountain high, disappear before the wind of God's
Spirit and we find that that which seemed so impreg-
nable was but a heap of chaff after all ! Many of us
are like the old woman who used to say, " I have had
many troubles during my life, but most of them never
came ! "

One further process is necessary before the grain
can be ground into flour. Having been threshed in
such a primitive manner, the grain contains dust from
the threshing-floor, small stones, damaged grains as
well as the seeds of many wild grasses, including,
more often than not, darnel, that unpleasant weed
which is rendered " tares " in Matthew xiii. 24-30.

Since neither the farmer nor the corn merchant
cleans the corn this has to be done by each household
as the grain is required. A sieve is used for this
purpose and the woman, for this work is always done
by women, sits on the floor and half fills the sieve with
wheat. To commence she shakes the sieve " from
right to left six or seven times, till all the crushed

straw and the chaff that still remain in the corn come to the surface, most of which she is able to gather up and throw away. Then she commences to hold the sieve in a slanting position, and for a considerable length of time jerks it up and down, blowing vigorously across it all the while with her mouth."* This causes the dust and fine grass seeds to fall through the meshes of the sieve, while the blowing disperses the remaining pieces of crushed straw. Finally she carefully goes over the corn, picking out any impurities which may still remain.

The tares, when growing, are so like the wheat that it is, even to-day, impossible to separate them. Both therefore have to be left to "grow together until the time of the harvest" (Matt. xiii. 30). Even then, during the threshing, some seeds of the tares will get among the wheat, and as the taste is very bitter, and when eaten separately or even diffused in ordinary bread it causes dizziness and often acts as a violent emetic, the seeds have to be picked out carefully grain by grain or else the flour will be unhealthy.

* " Everyday Life in the Holy Land," James Neil, M.A.

CHAPTER X

Eastern Customs of the Bible

PART II.—HOME LIFE

MOST people are interested in another's home life. Who does not turn for another glimpse of somebody's life as revealed by the lighted room, the curtains of which have not been drawn? Most people live two lives; one lived in the presence of the world and the other, which is the natural expression of what they are, lived in the unguarded atmosphere of the home. I remember reading the remarks of a certain curate who claimed that everyone had a false face and said that his were three well-defined ones. For convenience he named these the " pious-genteel " face for tea parties; the " hearty Christian " face for boys' and men's clubs, which necessitated the looking up of sports data; and the " bright boy of the village " face for mothers' meetings, to bring a little ray of sunshine (godly sunshine, of course) into their harassed lives.

While not endorsing these statements, it yet reveals to us the probable reason for the interest that the home-life of other people holds for us. It shows them with the mask off! A young man once came tremblingly to see his pastor. Listening to him in his pulpit utterances he had formed the opinion of an austere character far removed from the trials and difficulties of everyday life. Admitted to the manse, he was shown into the living room where he saw the minister on the floor pretending to be a horse while his children clambered over him, shouting with glee. He said afterwards that that touch of humanity had

made it so much easier for him to unburden his heart
—he felt that here was someone who would understand.

In order that we, too, may understand the men and
women of Bible days let us take a glimpse at them
in their homes and see them as they were.

The houses of the fellahin were simple one-roomed
structures having a flat roof, reached by steps outside. The interior, bare of any furniture save sometimes a raised stone platform which served as a couch
or bed at night, was usually lighted only by the door-
way, few Eastern houses, at least among the poorer
class, having windows. This one room served as the
day and night quarters for the whole family, while
often, stepped down a little, was a lower portion used
as a stable for the ass. It was probably in this lower
stable part in the house of some poor fellah at
Bethlehem that Jesus was born. The inn, where
naturally strangers would lodge the night, was on this
occasion full and therefore Joseph had to find shelter
elsewhere.

One piece of furniture would be found in every home ;
the grindstone wherewith to grind the daily ration
of flour. " At or before dawn every morning the
ringing, unmistakable sound of this grinding is heard
coming from every house. . . . And when ' the voice
[or sound] of the grinding is low ' (Eccles. xii. 4)
it is a sign that the family is impoverished, for bread
is their principal food."*

At night the whole family slept together in this
one-roomed house. They did not, and even now
wherever the ancient customs are preserved they
still do not, undress on lying down to sleep but simply
unloosed their girdles and removed their shoes. For
bedclothes they used their " Aba " or outer garment
of goat's or camel's hair-cloth. This garment, according to the Law, if taken in pledge was not to be

---

* " Everyday Life in the Holy Land," James Neil, M.A.

retained by the creditor over night for otherwise the debtor's night covering would be lacking to him (Exodus xxii. 26).

The bed consisted of a thin, lightly stuffed mattress which could be easily rolled up and put away in a closet during the day. It was usual to carry the sick on these light beds and therefore when the man who was sick of the palsy was healed by Jesus it would be quite simple for him to roll up his bed and carry it away under his arm.

The excuse, given by the friend at midnight, that he was with his children in bed and therefore could not rise to get the required loaves of bread seems to western ears rather strange, and so it would have been had the children been occupying a separate room. Since, however, they were all sleeping on the floor around him in true oriental fashion, to arise, get the bread and unbolt the door would therefore mean disturbing the sleep of the whole family (Luke xi. 7).

At night a lamp was kept burning as the Eastern had a horror of darkness. No matter how poor the family might be, they had a light all night. The reason for this custom was chiefly their dread of evil spirits which they believed were thus kept away. Among the virtues of the good wife, treasured and trusted by her husband, was the fact that her candle (lamp) went not out by night (Prov. xxxi. 18).

This is usually taken to mean that she diligently worked all night for her family. In an earlier verse we read that " she riseth also while it is yet night and giveth meat to her household " and I remember one virtuous mother in Israel questioning whether the model wife would, under the circumstances, be able to sleep at all ! In the East, however, no work was done after dark. Indeed, the feeble flickering light of the little oil lamp did not permit it, so that this cannot be the meaning of this passage. It rather means that so carefully did she clean and replenish the lamp that her family was never left in the darkness, and thus to their mind exposed to evil, during the night. Since these lamps were very small and needed attention every hour or so it would certainly mean that she had constantly to awake and refill the lamp lest it should go out and leave the family to the horror of darkness. This lamp stood on a lampstand where it literally gave light to all that were in the house through the hours of night (Matt. v. 15).

One of the evidences of God's watchful care for Israel in the wilderness was in the provision of a pillar of fire by night. As, in the desert, they had no means of obtaining oil the darkness would have been a continual source of fear had it not been for this miraculous provision by the loving Father-heart of God. How blessed, too, would be the promise of Jehovah to those who trusted in Him. "Thou shalt not be afraid for the terror by night" (Psalm xci. 5).

But what about their meals? What did they eat and how? In the centre of the floor, in the colder winter months, a fire would be kept burning throughout the day. Since there was no chimney the smoke soon filled the house, its only means of exit being a few holes over the door. Hence eyes, nostrils, and throat speedily became filled in a truly torturing fashion. The force of this is felt when God reproves the self-righteous, saying, " These are a smoke in My nose, a fire that burneth all the day " (Isaiah lxv. 5).

There were no chairs in the fallahin houses, for far simpler methods prevailed amongst the " common people " than amongst the belladin or townspeople. The latter, in the time of Christ, reclined at meals whereas the simple " fellah " sat on the floor, at a low table, with his feet tucked under him. He was careful not to show the sole of his foot for this was considered the height of indecorum.

The bread used was a pancake-like loaf of toasted whole wheat or barley meal about half an inch thick and about nine inches in diameter. Since leaven was more or less of a luxury, when Jesus referred to the leaven of the Pharisees, His simple disciples, nearly all fellahin, would naturally suppose Him to be warning them against the luxurious loaves found only in the houses of the rich townsmen.

The evening meal of the fellah was a simple one. It consisted of a stew which was placed upon the low table in one large dish from which each member of the family picked out an appetising morsel for himself.

Throughout the East, both rich and poor ate with their fingers and never used knife or fork. Since they dipped their hands into the common dish there arose the necessity for the washing of the hands before a meal. However, as this was merely a ceremonial act and consisted simply of the pouring of water over the hands, without any rubbing with soap or other cleanser, the hands were little the cleaner afterwards. Therefore, the Pharisees, when they commented upon the fact that the disciples washed not their hands before eating bread, were straining at a gnat and swallowing a camel as Christ promptly pointed out to them (Matt. xv. 1-20).

Upon the table there would also be placed some loaves of bread. These were never cut with a knife, as it was thought to be wicked to put a knife to it. When Christ fed the five thousand He " broke and gave the loaves to His disciples," and again when the Lord's supper was instituted He " took bread and blessed, and brake, and gave it to them " (Luke xxiv. 30).

In order to assist in eating, this bread was broken deftly into three-cornered pieces and bent into the shape of a spoon. With this the fellah was enabled to pick up some dainty piece from the common dish and since, having touched his mouth, etiquette demanded that the same " spoon " should not be used again both morsel and " spoon " were eaten.

This dipping into the dish is referred to by Jesus when He replied to the question of His disciples as to who should betray Him, " He that dippeth his hand with Me in the dish, the same shall betray Me " (Matt. xxvi. 23).

On any occasion when the host desired to show some special mark of his love and interest towards one of his guests he, instead of eating the morsel he had lifted on his bread spoon, would put this into the mouth of the favoured one. In the light of this, how solemn is that last scene when Jesus, wishing to give an especial sign to Judas of His love for him, bestowed upon him the sop after He had dipped it into the dish and lifted therefrom a delicious morsel.

CHAPTER XI.

Eastern Customs of the Bible

PART III.—BIBLE CHARACTERS

EVERY country has its own peculiar characters. I remember the surprise with which I learned that the blacking and polishing of shoes was, in America, a recognised trade having its own " shoeshine " parlours. There one climbs to a high throne, putting one's shoes on pedestals about three feet high, while the coloured shoe-shine man proceeds to put such a gloss upon them as I have seldom seen in this country.

Palestine is not without its special characters too, and we will in this chapter take a glimpse at a few of them.

Imagine a hot Eastern sun beating down from a pitilessly blue sky; dust clouds continually rising from scurrying feet; crowds jostling and pushing in the narrow streets; around one the bright colours of the Orient.

Look! Here comes the " sakkah " or water-seller, carrying on his back a large earthen jar, or perhaps a skin bottle, in which is the living water he has carried from some far distant spring or well. He cries out as he goes, " Ho, ye thirsty ones, come ye and drink!" and on this hot day he will sell many a cup of cool water to thirsty purchasers. Sometimes, when a rich man wishes to perform an act of charity he will pay for all the water contained in the water-carrier's bottle; this will then be distributed freely to the poor. The cry of the water-seller then will be changed to " Ho, ye thirsty ones, come and drink to-day for nothing."

With a rush the thirsty crowd will gather around, drinking thankfully the cool draught, and inquiring who the generous one might be; many will be the praises bestowed upon him for his kindness to the poor. Does not all this remind us of the words of Isaiah when he would introduce to us the water of everlasting life?

> " Ho everyone that thirsteth,
>   Come ye to the waters,
> And he that hath no money;
>   Come ye, buy and eat."
>   (Isaiah lv. 1).

But now, what is this curious sight? A huge box, seemingly many times too heavy for a man to lift, being borne along by a stooping figure. Ah! he is the "atal," the porter or burden-bearer, and it is amazing the size and weight of the burdens he can lift and carry for miles. He only uses a length of rope, knotted at one end, which he will throw around the load to evenly distribute its weight; stooping down and expelling his breath with a grunt, he will rise with a sudden spring, bringing the whole weight to bear upon his shoulders.

Should he stumble and fall the weight will go over his head, almost certainly breaking his neck. While the "atal" can lift excessively heavy loads, he cannot set them down again but has to be helped by another. David, complaining of his sins, likened them to this burden in these words, "For mine iniquities are gone over mine head, as an heavy burden they are too heavy for me " (Psalm xxxviii. 4).

Bunyan, in *Pilgrim's Progress,* has drawn his idea of the burden of sin from this passage, though many pictures showing Christian with his burden make it little larger than a knapsack which any hiker of to-day carries without difficulty. It was something much more cumbersome, heavy and unwieldy that David had in mind when he wrote of *his* burden!

Christ, too, when He would reprove the Pharisees, said of them, " They bind heavy burdens and grievous to be borne, and lay them on men's shoulders; but they themselves will not move them with one of their fingers " (Matt. xxiii. 4).

The burden of outward reformation without the change of heart is surely a grievous one, but what a change when, under the power of the new birth, the inner man is strengthened with all might. In contrast to this bondage, Christ's burden is a light one (Matt. xi. 30).

But who is this proud and haughty stranger? He seems to bring with him a breath of the open spaces! Ah, he is a bedouin and proudly feels himself superior to the townsmen. It is not difficult to recognise him by his head-dress, consisting mainly of a large, flowing, coloured scarf of silk or cotton.

Another distinguishing mark of the bedouin is the long sleeve, sometimes extending quite a yard beyond the length of his arm. When he is engaged in work or preparing for war he ties these sleeves together in a knot and throws them over his head out of the way. This leaves his arms bare and free. When, therefore, Isaiah would graphically describe the Lord, standing prepared to defend His people, he wrote, "Jehovah hath made bare His holy arm " (Isaiah lii. 10).

Our stranger carries, you will notice, a rough undressed bough of a tree called in the Hebrew " matteh." This is his badge of office as chieftain of his clan; it has descended from father to son and is hereditary.

When Moses met God at the burning bush, the Lord asked him, " What is that in thine hand? And he said, ' A matteh.' " (Exod. iv. 2). This staff became the wonder-working rod in the hands of Moses by which the " mattehs " of Pharaoh's magicians were swallowed up. In the wilderness, this rod budded, blossomed, and bare almonds to evidence God's choice of Aaron's priesthood.

Of Christ's priesthood, the Lord has promised He shall be a " Priest for ever after the order of Melchizedek " (Psalm cx. 4). And of this Kingly-Priest the Psalmist says, " The Lord shall send thy mighty ' matteh ' out of Zion " (Psalm cx. 2).

Since the " matteh " was the sign of authority as well as of priesthood it is most fittingly said to be given to Him who is not only now our High Priest but who will soon come to reign as King over all the earth. Just as Aaron's " matteh " came to life to prove his priesthood so too it is prophetically intimated that Christ's High-Priesthood would be proved by a still more wonderful miracle, namely, by His own body coming to life again on the third day after having been laid up before the Lord in that tomb just outside Jerusalem.

But now, coming towards us, I can see a figure clothed in a weather-worn jacket of sheep-skin, a club hanging from his girdle and a crook in his hand. He is, one would judge from his appearance, a shepherd and is perhaps on holiday to-day, having left his sheep in the hands of a keeper.

The work of looking after the sheep is usually, in the East, given to slaves or younger sons and sometimes to the daughters of the house ; Rachel was looking after her father's sheep when Jacob first met her beside the well (Gen. xxix. 9) ; David, the youngest son of Jesse, minded the sheep while the older sons took part in the fighting and hunting which were reckoned to be more honourable occupations ; and it is remarkable that the exception in the case of Jacob, where his eldest sons minded the sheep, while the youngest stayed at home, probably explains the reason for much of the jealousy shown by them to Joseph. Jacob reversed the general rule and custom and so aroused the hatred of the elder brothers.

The sheep-skin jacket our shepherd wears is the mark of a poor working man and this was, without doubt, why the writer to the Hebrews, in telling of the trials of the household of faith, said they " wandered about in sheep-skins, and goat-skins; being destitute, afflicted, tormented " (Heb. xi. 37).

Notice, too, the sling in the shepherd's hand. This is used as in this country we use the sheep-dog. Should one of the sheep begin to wander off the shepherd will sling a stone just beyond but without hitting it to frighten it into returning. Smooth stones are used such as can be found in the bed of some stream and these are kept in the shepherd's scrip or bag (I. Sam. xvii. 40). So accurate do they become in their aim that their marksmanship at short range equals that of an expert rifleman. David, who was no doubt proficient in the use of the sling, could therefore expect victory in his contest with Goliath for a stone slung at such close quarters would be quite sufficient to stun even a giant.

The club hanging from our shepherd's girdle is rendered " rod " in our Bible, while the crook is the " staff." The first was used to defend the sheep from wild beasts and robbers; the second for support in climbing the mountains. So beautifully does David apply this in the Shepherd Psalm, where he compares God's protection to the rod, and His support to the staff. " Thy rod and Thy staff they comfort me " (Psalm xxiii. 4).

But look! What is that man doing over there? Does he come into this busy street to write his letters? No! He is the scribe and that heavily veiled woman sitting beside him is, no doubt, whispering to him the message she wishes him to write for her. Very few in the East, until recently, could read or write and hence the necessity for official scribes. He carries his ink-horn in his girdle, you will notice, and he will put many a profuse oriental compliment in the letter he is writing. If you desire your letter to be respectful you must take a large sheet of paper and the lines should incline upward toward the left corner of the paper. When finished it must be put

in an envelope and sealed. The open letter, therefore, sent by Sanballat to Nehemiah was an insult
(Neh. vi. 5).

Just across the street can be seen a lad, carrying
on his head a tray with some small pancake-like
loaves. He is the baker's boy and as in the day of
Christ, he has some pieces of fried fish, too, upon his
tray. Probably that lad had sold most of his wares
when Andrew found him since there were only "five
barley loaves and two small fishes" left (John vi. 9). In
the hands of Christ, however, those few loaves became sufficient for the needs of the hungry multitude.

CHAPTER XII

MARTYRS OF THE BIBLE

THE romantic story of the Bible would not be complete did we not tell of those who courageously stood for its truths in the face of persecution and death. Wherever the Scriptures have gone some have found, mirrored in their depths, the eternal truths of the soul and spirit and, enraptured by this vision, the whole energies of the human heart have been called forth to spread the glorious message of Calvary. Contrariwise, others convicted but rebellious, have sought to smash the mirror which revealed their own degradation like the Hindu who gazed for the first time at some of the contaminated water of the Ganges under a powerful microscope, seeing its creeping abominations, smashed the instrument, foolishly considering it to be the source of the trouble instead of only the revealer of it. An infidel, loud-mouthed in his attacks upon the Bible, was once asked why he did not let it alone. His reply was self-revealing. " Because it will not let me alone ! "

So it has always been ! From the day when a king took a penknife and cut out those pages from the Word of God that were too disagreeable to him and consigned them to the fire (Jer. xxxvi. 23) to the present day when, less crudely but more surely, the Higher Critic and the Modernist deny its fundamental truths and emasculate its authority.

But it is not so much of its critics but of its defenders one would write and as the glorious roll of honour is unveiled may every heart burn with the desire to stand firm and true for the glorious truths of God's holy Word !

The Bible comes down to us through a line of crowned heads—but their crown was the crown of martyrdom !

Think then of the pagan persecutions against the Christians. Tacitus, the great Roman historian says that—

" Rome being set on fire, Nero declared it was the work of the Christians and put great numbers of them to death, after frightful tortures." Other heathen writers tell of the Christians as being " punished with the troublesome coat," which was made like a sack, of coarse cloth, besmeared with pitch, wax and sulphur : and being dressed in this coat, they were hung by their chins on sharp stakes fixed in the ground and then burnt—

" In that pitch'd shirt, in which such crowds expire,
    Chain'd to the bloody stake and wrapp'd in fire."

Nero had them burnt at midnight, " for torches," as he said, " to the city."*

During a later persecution at Cæsarea, in Palestine, a soldier named Marinus was called upon to own if his faith prevented him being advanced to the office of centurion. He confessed that he was a Christian and was then given three hours to recant. " His bishop, Theoctenes, took him by the hand and led him to their church, showed him the sword that hung by his side and a New Testament, which he took from his vest. Marinus stretched out his hand and clasped the Holy Scriptures.

" Hold fast," then said Theoctenes ; " cleave close to Him, whom you have chosen. You shall be strengthened by Him and depart in peace." After three hours he was beheaded, manfully confessing his faith in Christ."†

Many were the diabolical means adopted to stamp out Christianity. Houses were filled with Christians and then burnt to ashes. Companies of fifty were tied

---

* Quoted from " The Book and its Story."
† Quoted from Milner's " Church History."

together with ropes, and in droves were hurried into the sea. Swords, red-hot chairs, wheels for stretching human bodies, and talons of iron to tear them—all were the instruments of pagan Rome against the Christians. Yet still they would not give up the Book !

" Why," it was said to Euplius, a Sicilian martyr, " why do you not give up the Scriptures, as the Emperor has forbidden them? "

" Because," said he, " I am a Christian. Life eternal is in them. He who gives them up loses life eternal ! "*

The blood of the martyrs is, however, the seed of the Church, and in spite of all persecution and every effort to destroy the truth, the Word of God continued to exert its power to change the lives of even its persecutors and many a Saul of Tarsus became a Paul the apostle. Defeated, paganism retired crestfallen from the battlefield, but in her hour of triumph the Christian Church was beset by a more insidious foe. Ceremonialism and the traditions of men took the place of the unadulterated Word of God and thenceforward those who still retained the primitive faith were persecuted by those who claimed to be followers of the same Lord but whose ways were far from the simplicity of His gospel. Papal Rome took up the bloody sword which had fallen from the palsied arm of pagan Rome !

It is well to recall the fact that Britain was evangelised by primitive Christianity a long time prior to the papal mission of Augustine to Canterbury in A.D. 597. As early as the time of Paul's imprisonment in Rome the pure gospel was brought to these isles by a British prince named Caractacus and his father, Brân. They had been sent to Rome as hostages in the year A.D. 51 and stayed there seven years. Since during part of this time Paul was in Rome they, no doubt, heard the truth from his lips. The Welsh " triads " state that it was Brân who first brought

---

* Quoted from " The Book and its Story."

the Christian faith to the Cymry, or Welsh.* More swiftly than the dominion of the emperors there spread over these islands the dominion of the gospel and even in the wild parts of Scotland were heard the songs of the redeemed.

From Scotland there went to Ireland, in the year 388, a boy named Succat, who was afterwards to be known as St. Patrick. At first a slave there, sent into the green pastures of Ireland to keep swine, he afterwards preached the gospel to the Irish pagans, calling them to meeting by the beat of the drum. Many were converted and Ireland after this period became known as the " Isle of Saints."

Two centuries later, Columba, of Ireland, repaid the debt and set out to preach the gospel in Scotland. From Iona, which became the seat of this new mission, the Picts of Scotland were evangelised.

Then, in 597, Augustine came to England in an endeavour to place the chains of the Romish Church upon the free spirits of the British Christians. To all his efforts to persuade them to acknowledge the supremacy of the Pope they replied saying, " they knew no other Master but Christ." Said Augustine, " If you will not unite with us in showing the Saxons the way of life, you shall receive from them the stroke of death." Argument had failed : now for the sword !†

Shortly after the death of Augustine, one of the Anglo-Saxon kings, named Edelfrid, attacked these British Christians. " Twelve hundred and fifty servants of the living God, calling to mind what are the arms of Christian warfare, after preparing themselves by fasting, met together in a retired spot to send up their prayers to God." Edelfrid commanded his soldiers to fall upon the praying crowd and twelve hundred of them were slain. " Thus did Rome loose the savage pagan against the primitive Church of

---

* Quoted from " The Book and its Story."

† D'Aubigne's " History of the Reformation."

H

Britain and fasten it all dripping with blood to her triumphal car.''*

It would require more than one chapter to tell even a small part of the sufferings of Bible lovers of bygone days. All one can do is to draw aside the curtain for an occasional glance at the blood-stained stage and then let it drop again.

Look now at the Waldenses, inhabitants of the Alps. Their only fault, although a great one in the eyes of Rome, was the possession of a translation of parts of the Scriptures in their own native tongue. Since, in those days, there were no printing presses all copies of the Scriptures had to be handwritten, and were, therefore, very expensive. Since also their enemies seized and burnt every copy they could get hold of, the Waldenses formed societies of young persons, every member of which was trusted to preserve in his memory a certain number of chapters. When they assembled for worship these young people would recite, one after another, chapters from the priceless Book.

'' Flayed alive, and then crushed with heavy stones, cast down from towers, their flesh shredded with iron whips and then beaten to death with lighted brands . . . mothers and children driven up by hundreds to perish in the upper snows, their flesh cut alive from their bones . . . their spirit of endurance spoke in the words of one of their heroic pastors, ' You will sooner want wood wherewith to burn us, than men ready to burn in witness of their faith : from day to day we multiply and the Word of God endureth for ever.' ''†

Wickliffe, the '' Morning star of the Reformation,'' and the translator of the Scriptures into the English tongue, was spared the martyr's end although, after his death, his body was exhumed and burnt to ashes. His followers, who were called Lollards, were subjected, however, to all the pent-up hatred of the enemies of the open Bible. A pious clergyman in London,

---

* D'Aubigne's '' History of the Reformation.''
† Quoted from '' The Book and its Story.''

William Sawtre by name, who openly taught the doctrines of Wickliffe, had presumed to say, " Instead of adoring the cross on which Christ suffered, I adore Christ who suffered on it." For this saying he was burnt alive at Smithfield in March, 1401. Many others were imprisoned and the Lollards' tower in the Bishop's palace at Lambeth was soon filled with those whose only fault was a love for the Scriptures. Many carved upon the walls of their dungeons the expression of their sorrow and their hopes : *" Jesus amor meus,"* wrote one, which being interpreted means, " Jesus is my love."*

Next listen to the story of an earnest Christian named John Brown, of Ashford. In the spring of 1517 he travelled on board the passage-boat from London to Gravesend. Standing next him was a priest who insolently said : " You are too near me, get farther off. Do you know who I am?"

" No, sir," answered Brown.

" Well, then, you must know that I am a priest."

" Indeed, sir ; are you a parson, or vicar, or a lady's chaplain ? "

" No ; I am a soul-priest," he haughtily replied, " I sing mass to save souls."

" Do you, sir," rejoined Brown somewhat ironically, " that is well done ; and can you tell me where you find the soul when you begin the mass ? "

" I cannot," said the priest.

" And where you leave it when the mass is ended ? "

" I do not know."

" What ! " continued Brown with marks of astonishment, " you do not know where you find the soul or where you leave it, . . . and yet you say that you save it ! "

The priest became very angry and threatened vengeance. Later Brown was apprehended for it was a serious matter to jest with a priest ! Brought before the Archbishop he was commanded to acknowledge the

* D'Aubigne's " History of the Reformation."

efficacy of the mass, but Brown answered, " Christ was once offered to take away the sins of many. It is by this sacrifice we are saved, and not by the repetitions of the priests."

At this reply a pan of burning coals was brought in, one took off his shoes and stockings and compelled him to stand on the live coals until the flesh was burnt off the soles of his feet even to the bones. Still he remained unshaken. His tormentors therefore delivered him over to the civil powers to be burnt alive.

Led back to Ashford, he was put in the stocks where his wife Elizabeth found him, his features changed by suffering. The poor woman sat down beside him, weeping most bitterly. Said he: " I cannot set my feet to the ground for bishops have burnt them to the bones; but they could not burn my tongue and prevent me confessing the Lord. . . . O Elizabeth! . . . continue to love Him for He is good; and bring up our children in His fear." The following day he was burned to death.*

The same spirit which upheld John Brown enabled Luther to face the august assembly of the Diet of Worms before which he had been cited to appear. Kindly friends warned him. " They will burn you and reduce your body to ashes," they said. But nothing frightened Luther. " though they should kindle a fire," said he, " all the way from Worms to Wittemburg, the flames of which reached to heaven, I would walk through it in the name of the Lord. . . . "

Later another sympathiser tried to prevent his entry into Worms. Luther answered that " even should there be as many devils in Worms as tiles on the housetops, still I would enter it! "

When, before the Diet, it was demanded of him that he should retract his writings he answered, " Unless I am convinced by the testimony of Scriptures . . . I cannot and I will not retract, for it is unsafe for a Christian to speak against his conscience." Then look-

* D'Aubigne's " History of the Reformation."

ing round on this assembly before which he stood, and which held his life in its hands, he said : " Here I stand, I can do no other ; may God help me ! Amen !"*

Although Luther was not himself martyred for his faith in Christ and his courageous stand for the Word of God, yet many of his followers suffered in this way. At Buda, in Hungary, there was an evangelical bookseller named John who had circulated Luther's New Testament and other of his writings throughout that country. He was apprehended and bound to the stake ; his persecutors piled his books around him, enclosing him as if in a tower and then set fire to them. " John manifested unshaken courage, exclaiming from the midst of the flames that he was delighted to suffer in the cause of the Lord. ' Blood follows blood,' cried Luther, when informed of this martyrdom, ' but that generous blood, which Rome loves to shed, will at last suffocate the Pope with his kings and their kingdoms.' "*

Fanaticism grew fiercer every day. Lutherans were hanged and ruffians were even found who unfeelingly nailed the pastors by their tongues to a post; so that these unhappy victims, tearing themselves violently from the wood to which they were fastened, were horribly mutilated in attempting to recover their liberty, and thus deprived of that gift which they had long used to proclaim the gospel.*

In spite, however, of every persecution the Word of God triumphed gloriously. Truth is so precious that men will rather die than part with it. The wondrous power of the Word is evidenced in the conversions of Thomas Bilney and through him of Hugh Latimer, both of whom were afterwards martyred for their faith.

Bilney, during his studies at Cambridge, came under deep conviction of sin. Anxious about his salvation, he applied to the priests, whom he looked upon as physicians of the soul. Kneeling before his confessor,

---

* D'Aubigne's " History of the Reformation."

with humble look and pale face, he told him all his sins. The priest prescribed at one time fasting, at another prolonged vigils, and then masses and indulgences, which cost him dearly. Although he went through all these penances with great devotion, they brought him no peace of mind and being of a weak constitution his body wasted away by degrees. "Alas!" said Bilney in anguish, "my last state is worse than the first."

One day he heard some friends talking about the Greek Testament of Erasmus. Feeling that God might have placed therein some word which perhaps would heal his soul, he slipped into the house where the volume was secretly sold, bought it with fear and trembling and then hastening to his own room, shut the door. As he opened the book his eyes caught these words :

" This is a faithful saying, and worthy of all acceptation, that Christ Jesus came into the world to save sinners : of whom I am chief." (I. Tim. i. 15). This message brought light to his darkened mind and it seemed to him as if a refreshing wind were blowing over his soul.

" I also am like Paul," exclaimed he with emotion, " and more than Paul, the greatest of sinners ! . . . But Christ saves sinners. At last I have heard of Jesus."*

Doubts ended, Bilney was saved. An unknown joy pervaded him and instead of despair he felt an inward peace. Thereafter he began to speak and to preach of the grace that had saved him. But God destined him to be the instrument in the conversion of one who was to become a champion more illustrious than himself.

There was in Cambridge at that time a priest notorious for his ardent fanaticism against the evangelical truths which Bilney and his friends were teaching. His name was Hugh Latimer, and he en-

---

* D'Aubigné quoting Foxe.

deavoured in every way to hinder the cause of the gospel. As he himself afterwards confessed, " I was then as obstinate a papist as any in England."*

During one of his pulpit discourses, in which he was especially virulent, Bilney was among his hearers and conceived the design of winning Latimer to the gospel. But how to manage it? The prejudiced Latimer would not listen to any reasoning or argument. Praying about the matter Bilney thought of a strange plot. He went to Latimer one day and said to him, " For the love of God be pleased to hear my confession." The ardent Latimer, thinking that Bilney was about to renounce his belief in the Scriptures and return to the fold of the Roman Church, gladly consented.

Kneeling before the priest, Bilney related to him with touching simplicity the anguish he had once felt in his soul, the efforts he had made to remove it, their unprofitableness so long as he determined to follow the precepts of the Church and lastly, the peace he had felt when he believed that Jesus Christ is the Lamb of God that taketh away the sins of the world. He described to Latimer the spirit of adoption he had received and the happiness he experienced in being able to call God his Father. . . . As Latimer listened the Holy Ghost spoke to him through the simple words of the humble disciple and Hugh Latimer was converted. It was not the penitent, but the confessor, who received absolution and Latimer, viewing with horror his previous persecutions of the believers, wept bitterly. Bilney, however, consoled him. " Brother," said he, " though your sins be as scarlet, they shall be white as snow."*

So another captive of Satan was freed and his chains of superstition broken by the wondrous Sword of the Spirit. From this time on Latimer became a mighty defender of the Truth. Some years later, in 1531, Bilney was burned at the stake. Latimer, however,

---

* D'Aubigné quoting Foxe.

in spite of his opinions and principally because his sermons inculcated practical righteousness, (although as he stated them they were diametrically opposed to the prevailing errors of the times, yet could scarcely be controverted), lived to become Bishop of Worcester.

During the reign of Mary, in 1555, he and Ridley were led to the stake at Oxford. Free from taint of fanaticism, Latimer met death with a calmness and a courage which enabled him to taste in dying an ineffable thrill of victorious achievement. Turning to Ridley he said, " Be of good comfort, Master Ridley, and play the man; we shall this day light such a candle by God's grace in England as I trust shall never be put out." A chronicler says he " received the flame as it were embracing it. After he had stroked his face with his hands and as it were bathed them a little in the fire, he soon died as it appeared with very little pain or none."

This chapter must close with an account of the fate of Ann Askew. In the year 1540 there might have been seen in the crypt of St. Paul's Church a company of people gathered to hear the reading of a copy of the " Great Bible," so called because of its size, which was chained to one of the pillars. The reader's name was Porter : he was chosen as reader because he could read well and had an audible voice. So many listened to him that he was brought before Bishop Bonner and accused of making tumults. Bonner sent him to Newgate, where, for teaching his fellow-prisoners what he had learned in the Scriptures, he was laid in the lower dungeon of all, fastened by his neck to the wall and was so oppressed with bolts and irons that, in eight days, this tall, strong young man was found dead.

Amongst his regular hearers was Ann Askew; she had been turned out of doors by her husband for studying the Word of God. Some time after this she was called before Bonner and told, without any trial, that she should be burnt. " I have searched all Scripture," she said in reply, " yet could I never find that either

Christ or His apostles put any creature to death.''
Later they put her on the rack. Telling of this afterwards she said :

" Then they did put me on the rack, because I
confessed no ladies or gentlemen to be of my opinion,
and thereon they kept me for a long time; and because I lay still and did not cry, my Lord Chancellor
Wriothesley and Mr. Rich took pains to rack me well-
nigh dead; then the lieutenant, Sir Anthony Knevett,
caused me to be loosed, and I swooned, and then they
recovered me again. After that I sat two long hours,
reasoning with my Lord Chancellor, on the bare floor,
where he with many flattering words, persuaded me
to alter my opinion; then was I brought to a house
and laid on a bed, with as weary and painful bones as
ever had patient Job.''*

Three days later Ann, whose bones were all dis-
located, was carried in a chair to Smithfield and burned
at the stake. When, before the flames were kindled,
she was presented with a pardon if she would recant
she bravely replied : "I came not hither to deny my
Lord and Master.'' And so another martyr's crown
was won !

But space would fail to tell of all who sealed their
testimony in their blood. The histories of the few
given here should surely arouse us to a greater love
and a nobler defence of those Scriptures for which they
bled and died. Shall we prove unfaithful to the trust
handed to us in hands licked by the flames? God
forbid ! Resist then, with all the God-given strength
ye have, every effort of Satan to hinder the power of
the Word of God, whether by direct opposition or by
the more subtle and indirect way of careless indifference. Prize the prize handed to us over the
tortured, racked, flame-consumed bodies of those saints
of whom the world was not worthy !

---

* Quoted from " The Book and its Story.''

CHAPTER XIII

Romance in the Bible

I T would be strange if we did not devote one chapter
to telling of the romance in the Bible, especially
as there is something about a love story which
interests everyone. Accordingly, let us look for a
while at the Eastern customs of courtship and marriage
and see in what way these throw light upon the sacred
Scriptures.

In the East everyone is expected to marry, and a
Mahommedan nobleman would, if it were necessary,
call a beggar out of the street to marry his daughter
rather than have her unmarried. Further, no one
chooses his or her own partner; the woman is " given
in marriage " and the man has his bride chosen for
him. Although to our Western ideas this seems scarcely fair to those most concerned it is noteworthy that
few marriages in the East turn out unhappily, and as
the elders were able to choose without the traditional
blindness of love to hamper them, their choice was
usually a good one. It is true that the young people
could not be in love with one another at the time of
the marriage but in the East this was not thought to
be necessary as they said, " Love comes after marriage, not before." Indeed, even with us, does not
the highest and holiest love, built upon a fuller understanding of each other, come after marriage?

The choosing of a bride was usually undertaken by
the women of the family and a man's wife was chosen
by his mother and his aunts. Much care was taken
over the selection, far more than is to-day usually
exercised by young men on their own behalf. When
a choice had been made, the female relatives of the

young man paid a morning call at the prospective bride's home and expressed the object of their visit by asking for " a glass of water at the hands of the daughter of the house."* She, hurriedly dressed for the occasion in her best attire, would then come in and wait, serving a light repast. When finally the coffee had been passed around she would retire and a proposal would be made for her and her price discussed. According to the invariable Eastern custom, Christ is said to have bought His Bride, the Church; and at what a price, too, for He paid for her with His own life's blood on Calvary (Acts xx. 28).

It was, perhaps, just as well a man had to buy his wife in the East, for otherwise the lot of the poor despised girls would have been even harder to bear than it was. Few people would care to tell an Oriental father in public that a daughter was born to him, and if a slave were sent to tell the news he would say, " A son is born to you, my lord." This, because he would be ashamed to tell his lord publicly of anything so humiliating as the birth of a girl! Should you ask a man how many children he had he would reply, " The Lord hath given to thy servant four children," that is, giving the number of his sons only and ignoring altogether the existence of his four or five daughters. A man will say to a doctor, " Sir, I have a sick man at my house; please come and see him," and the experienced medical man replies, " Yes, I will come and see her," for he knows it is his wife whom he has been ashamed to mention.* Girls in the East well know this humiliating fact and have a phrase to express anything that is trifling, " It is as small as the rejoicing the day I was born."

But the despised girls are worth a good sum to their father in the way of purchase money from prospective sons-in-law and many a man is set up in business in the East by money borrowed from a money-lender on

---

* " Everyday Life in the Holy Land," James Neil, M.A.

the security of the purchase money he hopes to receive for his daughters when they become of the age to be married! In the time of Moses the "dowry of virgins" appears to have been reckoned for general purposes at "fifty shekels of silver" (Exod. xxii. 16, 17, with Deut. xxii. 28, 29). This sum would amount to about £6 but would, of course, buy much more than that sum would to-day. Jacob, not having any money to buy his bride, offered to work seven years for her, and thus, whatever was the wage of a man in those days, paid a very much higher price for Rachael.

All preliminary arrangements having been made, the day of the marriage arrived. In Bible lands the marriage ceremony was of the simplest and consisted merely of the receiving of the bride into the bridegroom's house, this being an acknowledgment before witnesses that he took her as his wife. However, the processions and entertainments in connection with it were most elaborate. These rejoicings continued for seven days and sometimes even for twice that period. At Samson's nuptials the festivities lasted seven days, during which time the Philistines attempted to guess his riddle (Judges xiv. 12). Lavish hospitality was indulged in at these times, open house was kept, and passers-by as well as friends were invited to the feast. This will explain the reason for the shortage of wine at the feast of Cana of Galilee and also the great quantity of wine miraculously supplied by Christ, amounting in all to some sixty gallons, when

> The conscious water saw its God
> And blushed.

It should be borne in mind that the best wine in Palestine is the pure fermented juice of the grape quite unfortified and containing little percentage of alcohol. Since also all wine throughout the East, when drunk, is mixed with about half its bulk of water its strength would be almost negligible. Remembering also the crowds that attend a marriage it will be seen that this bounteous provision of wine by Christ would not tend in any way to excessive drinking.

Towards the close of the feasting and rejoicing came the actual wedding. This took place at midnight. The bridegroom's procession set out for the home of the bride, the bridegroom attired in a rich cloak and new clothes and seated upon a white horse. How true is the type to the reality !

" And I saw heaven opened and behold a white horse ; and He that sat upon him was called Faithful and True " (Rev. xix. 11). " And at midnight there was a cry made, Behold, the Bridegroom cometh " (Matt. xxv. 6).

The procedure of the marriage was somewhat as follows. The bridegroom was accompanied by his groomsmen, called in the Scriptures the "companions" (Judges xiv. 11), and was preceded by a band of musicians or singers (Jer. vii. 34), and by persons bearing flambeaux or lighted torches (Rev. xviii. 23). Having reached the home of the bride, who with her maidens had been anxiously expecting his arrival, the bridegroom conducted the whole party back to his own, or his father's, house with every demonstration of gladness.

" With gladness and rejoicing shall they be brought : They shall enter into the King's palace " (Psa. xlv. 15).

" In My Father's house are many mansions . . . I go to prepare a place for you. . . . I will come again, and receive you unto Myself " (John xiv. 2, 3).

So will our heavenly Bridegroom come for His Church and bring her into His Father's house. Glad will be the day when we shall see Him coming with power and great glory.

On their way back to the bridegroom's house, the party was joined by the maidens, friends of the bride and bridegroom, who were waiting to join the procession as it passed. The Oriental has many charming exhibitions of hospitality and none is so delightful as the custom of going out, often for many miles, to meet, welcome, and escort to the journey's end a coming visitor. Hence it will be well understood that, when the bridegroom was about to return with his bride, the rites of hospitality required that friends should go out to meet him. Wearied by the entertaining and the un-accustomed late hour, the women naturally fall asleep but are awakened by the near approach of the proces-sion and the cry : " Behold, the bridegroom cometh ! "

An ancient police regulation forbade anyone going out at night without carrying a light. This is still, in all purely Oriental parts, a small oil lamp carried in a kind of rude Chinese lantern of paper or oiled silk. Since at that hour of the night it would be nearly impossible to obtain a fresh supply of oil, foolish virgins, without sufficient oil, would neither be able to take part in the procession nor go with the bridegroom into his house for the marriage supper.

The face of the Eastern bride was not seen by the prospective bridegroom until after they were married. Accordingly the greatest care was taken to prepare her so that when he lifted her veil to take his first look, the impression should be a favourable one. Her nails, hands, arms, breasts, and feet were stained with paste of henna. Her cheeks and lips were painted red ; her eyebrows pencilled so as to appear to meet—for beetle brows are thought beautiful in the East ! Her eyes were tinted black between the lids by a powder of smoke black so as to make them appear larger and brighter ; and the skin of her face was made smooth and shining as a piece of polished marble ! Thus Jezebel, when she looked out of the lattice " painted her face " (II. Kings ix. 30). The wedding garment of the bride was of the richest materials, embroidered with coloured silks, heavy gold and silver thread and glittering spangles.* To the Eastern mind no illus-tration of beauty and splendour could be greater than the words of Isaiah lxi. 10 : " He hath clothed me

---

* " Everyday Life in the Holy Land," James Neil, M.A.

with the garments of salvation . . . as a bride adorneth herself with her jewels."

So also, when the Apostle John sees the New Jerusalem, the future home of the Bride, coming down from heaven he sees it so adorned with jewels, sparkling and gleaming in the sunlight, that he describes it as " prepared as a bride adorned for her husband " (Rev. xxi. 2).

The story of Abraham's servant's search for a bride for Isaac (Genesis xxiv.) very beautifully illustrates Oriental marriage customs. When Abraham decided that it was time for Isaac to be married he did not send for him and communicate his thoughts on the subject to his son but instead called for the eldest servant in his house, probably Eliezer (Genesis xv. 2), and sent him into Mesopotamia to get a bride from his kindred there. Difficult enough was his task, for he, a man, had to negotiate a marriage—a duty which was usually left to the women. He had also to get a wealthy and influential family to forgo all the elaborate and joyful ceremonies connected with a wedding so dear to the women and in their eyes almost sacred. Lastly, he had to persuade the parents to permit a young girl to go away a journey of something over four hundred miles to be married to a strange man in a strange land.

Remarkably did the Lord answer the prayers of the old man and the first damsel to come to the well at which he rested was Rebekah. Then the negotiations began, and finally Eliezer was permitted to return with the bride for his master's son, Isaac. After the long, tiring tramp across the desert Rebekah saw Isaac meditating in the field and when she was informed who he was " she took a veil and covered herself."

" And she became his wife ; and he loved her : and Isaac was comforted after his mother's death " (Gen. xxiv. 65, 67).

What a beautiful type of the love of Christ for the Church ; Eliezer, the trusted messenger of Abraham, a picture of the Holy Spirit, Who has been sent forth by the heavenly Father to search out and bring home a Bride for His once-slain but now risen Son, and the love of Isaac for Rebekah is but a faint picture of the love of Christ for the redeemed.

How sublime and grand are the closing scenes of this age as chapter after chapter the romantic story of Christ's love for His Bride are unfolded! We have first the heavenly Lover gazing upon the damsel of His choice, not beautiful indeed, but covered with mire and clothed with filthy rags (Psalm xl. 2; Isaiah lxiv. 6), and with her face covered with putrifying sores (Isaiah i. 6). Her condition awakens in His pure heart a compassionate love and He determines to win her for His Bride.

The next chapter opens with a depth of sacrifice, so great that this world has never beheld its like before nor since. The only way to win her to Himself is for Him to bear her sins and pay the extreme penalty for her crimes. Surely here is where this idyll must be broken! Let romance then lift her pinions, take flight and leave the wretched one in her misery to meet the just penalty of her sins. Nay, stay! Behold! the heavenly Lover dies to save the object of His choice— every drop of blood that stains the sward of Golgotha's hill cries out His divine love and intention toward sinning humanity. Deathless in His love, rising triumphantly over every obstacle, He awaits the issue in His Father's house.

The following chapter tells of the love letters He sends, each phrase pulsating with the ardour of His divine passion. Surely when they read, their hearts will warm towards Him! Can they still remain cold and unaffected by such compassion? Strange, how strange, it is, but I must record the heart break of the story; she will not read His love letters, His Word, but tears them in pieces unread, and leaves His love unrequited and misunderstood.

Next I read of the heavenly Lover sending His Friend, the Holy Spirit, to persuade the foolish and self-willed damsel to return, in some measure, the ardour of His affection. Thank God, the efforts of this Friend are successful and, enraptured now that she understands a little of the love of her heavenly Lover, I see a marvellous change take place in the face and form of the damsel. The mud is cleansed away (I. John i. 7); the rags are now changed for a spotless robe (Rev. xix. 8); and gone are the sores of sin.

But she has not yet seen Him. Her Friend and His Friend, the Holy Spirit, has told her all about Him (John xvi. 14), and she has fallen in love with the description of her heavenly Lover (I. Peter i. 8). Comes His determination to return to the city of the Bride and to take her back with Him to His Father's house, where He has been preparing a home for her (John xiv. 2).

The great day, so long awaited by both, at last dawns. The heavens open and the wedding procession comes from the skies preceded by choirs of angels and the harps of heaven, playing the wedding march. Who is that in the forefront of the multitudes? He, Who is clothed in garments of light, shining with the glory of the sun, with eyes full of eager anticipation? 'Tis the Christ! Heart throbbing with emotion, the Bride goes forth to meet Him (I. Thess. iv. 16, 17), and as she gazes upon the face of her Beloved, the last remnants of the earthiness that so long prevented her accepting His love slips away and she is transfigured too, catching a little of the love-light in His eyes she becomes glorious to look upon even as He (Phil. iii. 21; I. John iii. 2).

The closing chapter tells us of the glad wedding day. Can mortal language speak of the scene as the Saviour takes the redeemed Church, which is His Bride, and presents her faultless before His Father in heaven? Can mortal eyes imagine the glorious scene as rank upon rank, tier upon tier, the angels witness the immortal nuptials? Can mortal ears imagine the ineffable strains of heavenly music that shall usher in the wedding party? Can mortal mind comprehend the glorious splendour of the home of the Bridegroom? Centuries has He been in preparing for this glad day and all the powers of Deity have been called into operation to make the future home of the Bridegroom and His Bride. So we must close this wonderful story with words often used before, but never so true as now, " and they lived happily ever after."

Should one read this who has not yet heeded the call of the Holy Spirit to become a member of the Bride of Christ, which is His Church, may I ask such an one the question asked of Rebekah—

" Wilt thou go with this Man? "

The Holy Spirit would lead you to Christ, who loves you and has bought you with His own precious blood. Accept Him to be your Saviour and Friend and say, as Rebekah did long ago, " I will go " (Gen. xxiv. 58).

CHAPTER XIV

THE SPIRITUAL VALUE OF THE BIBLE

HOW often the Bible is neglected though it contains a mine of intellectual and spiritual wealth for those who will dig for it. A remarkable story is told of an unrecognised gem. Gustaf Gillman, a Chicago lapidary, was working in his shop when a labourer named John Mihok entered and gave him a rough red stone to cut.

" Where did you get it? " gasped Gillman.

" My father picked it up in Hungary fifty years ago ! " replied Mihok. " He thought it was a pretty pebble. When I landed in this country I found it in my valise. It has been lying around the house ever since. The children played with it. My last baby cut his teeth on it. One night I dreamed it was a diamond and worth a lot of money ; but it's not a diamond. It's red."

" No," said Gillman. " It's a pigeon's-blood ruby."

" What might it be worth? " asked Mihok.

" I'd say anywhere from £20,000," replied Gillman.

How often, also, the priceless gem of the Word of God lies unrecognised and unread upon the bookshelf. Some while ago a journalist named Reginald Pound wrote of his rediscovery of its spiritual value. For years a family Bible, belonging to his grandfather and left to him in his will, had lain neglected. Once he came across it in the garage ; then it became an improvised cushion, covered with chintz, in an armchair ; again he discovered it being used as a table for a doll's tea party, to which his youngest children had invited him.

Taking it up he opened it casually and began to read, careless of his responsibilities as guest on this special occasion.   Opened at Psalm xlvi., he seemed to hear again the voice of his grandfather, long dead.

> " God is our refuge and strength,
>   A very present help in trouble.
> Therefore will not we fear,
>   Though the earth be removed,
> And though the mountains be carried
>   Into the midst of the sea ;
>
> God is in the midst of her ;
>   She shall not be moved ;
> God shall help her,
>   And that right early.''

He says, " I read Psalm liii. and felt humble.   I read Psalm cxxi. and tried to find out for myself the secret of its majesty.   Of course, it utterly eluded me. I read Psalm cxxxvii. and ached in my heart that I should never write like that, and was consoled only by thinking that no one else would either.   Then I read the Sermon on the Mount.   It seemed to me to have gathered new force in the years since I had last read it for myself.   Or is it that I had grown wiser and cast off some of my greater conceits.   Looking up presently I found that the children had gone . . . only myself and the Bible in the silent room.   It was a solemn moment. . . . I tell you there was peace in my soul when I put down the Bible.''

Still another writes of finding the Bible to be a great aid to devotion when he took it into the inner chamber.   He commenced with the Psalms.

" When I began I was called at five o'clock in the morning and had to be at work at six, so I read my morning portion the night before.   I read through the appointed portion in a prayerful spirit again and again, then went over it clause by clause on my knees, turning its statements into prayer and thanksgiving.

Then I wrote out the verse or phrase that spoke to me, read it over next morning as I dressed, committed the day briefly to God and put the text in my waist-coat pocket. Before I found this method I used to try to work myself into a praying mood, but I lacked resourcefulness and praying became ' prayers ' again and listening a void. Prayer has been an experience of thrilling wonder, creative meditation and real fellow-ship since it has been instructed, quickened, and in-spired by the Word of God. . . . I find it well to take the sayings of Psalmist and Prophet and turn them into prayers . . . the heart is soon aglow when the Word is alight."*

Summing up the facts of the previous chapters we see that the Bible is supernatural in its origin, for it is God-breathed (II. Tim. iii. 16). One recalls how one day a Swiss friend was trying to read a passage out of an English Bible : but the effort robbed the words of their sweetness and a well-used French Bible was lovingly turned to that the phrases familiar from childhood might again speak to the soul. Yet the Scriptures were written neither in English nor French ! A native of the Congo recently exclaimed, upon read-ing the same wonderful book in Kiluba, " It speaks ! " To him Jesus will ever speak nothing but pure Kiluba ! " Only the Divine origin of the Bible can adequately account for the fact that when translated into the strangest and most diverse languages it still lives and speaks from every line with gripping, compelling interest and power." Because the Bible is inspired, it inspires.

Then the Bible is complete in its structure for " the law of the Lord is perfect " (Psalm xix. 7-10). Not one book can be spared without a gap being left in a structure which is otherwise perfect. Just as the taking away of a stone from the wall of a building would leave an unsightly gap to mark the loss, so would the taking away of anything from the Scriptures.

---

* " The Path of Prayer," Samuel Chadwick.

The Bible is inerrant in its contents since it is " for ever settled in heaven " and is " very pure " (Psa. cxix. 89, 140).

Difficulties there may be and are, but these very difficulties prove it to be the Word of God. If the Bible could be easily comprehended by all it would be one of the surest proofs of its human origin. Since the greatest thinkers have been unable to plumb its depths while even the fool can understand its plain message we perceive the masterly hand of God.

" What the Bible is," writes Henry Ward Beecher, " is shown in the men who use it. It is not in the letter that the Word of God has power, but in the *spirit.*" Some come to the Bible solely to criticise and so they find much to criticise; others read it as literature (and it is great literature), and they see nothing more; others again read it as God's Word and they hear God speaking to them through its pages.

" But," says the critic, " is there not a great deal in the Bible that is useless—chaff and straw, as it were? " But what would the farmer do for wheat if he had the same contempt for the chaff and straw in April and May as he has in August or September? The wheat in spring is a little sucking babe and the straw is the full-breasted mother feeding the wheat; it is the mother's arm around it, protecting it. Since the Word of God was gradually constructed, bearing finally the full-eared wheat of the revelation of the Gospel in Christ, we honour those Old Testament roots upon which grew such glory.

The Bible is reliable in its promises, for we are assured all the promises of God are yea and amen in Christ Jesus (II. Cor. i. 20).

A vicar in the North once visited one of his parishioners, a very old lady. Wishing to read her a few verses, he picked up a Bible which lay on the table, and was puzzled to find on almost every page the two letters " T " and " P." " Why," he enquired gently, " have you so disfigured your Bible? "

" Disfigured it, sir? " she echoed. " It's no dis-figuring. These are the Lord's promises. ' T ' stands for ' Tested ' and ' P ' for ' Proved.' For a moment the vicar was taken aback. Then he said slowly, "I've read my Bible in the Hebrew and the Greek but now I think yours is the best way to read it."

A short while ago a famous American humorist said enthusiastically : " I read the Bible two hours a day ! How did I find time to do this? I will tell you. I began by reading fifteen minutes a day and this in-creased my general efficiency so much that I soon found I could give up an hour and lose nothing, but gain. Then I found I could give up another hour. The Bible . . . makes you cheerful, persistent, honest, and gives you the kind of an understanding that looks through a superficial proposition into the source. It gives you the spiritual power to know how to be pro-vided all the time with the right equipment to carry on your work."

The Bible is also faith-inspiring in its ministry for " faith cometh by hearing, and hearing by the Word of God " (Rom. x. 17).

It is said that Torrey once heard Moody preach on Faith. He went home determined to obtain more faith. His method was to try and arouse more faith in his own heart, but he found it a miserable failure, until one day in his reading of the Scripture he came across this verse, " Faith cometh by hearing, and hearing by the Word of God." This revolutionised Torrey's methods of obtaining faith, and thenceforward he found that the more he read and fed upon the Word of God the more his faith grew.

Someone asked the question : " When may a Chris-tian take a promise without presumption?" And the answer was, " When he takes *all* the Scripture and embraces it as spoken to him, then he may take any particular promise boldly."

Seth Joshua, the Welsh Evangelist, said, " From experience I find that freedom in prayer and readiness of matter depend largely upon Bible study. Communion with the written Word seems to be a staircase up to communion with the Living Word."

A pastor one day asked a member of his church how she was getting along in her Christian life.

" Very poorly," she replied, " my life is a disgrace to me, to the Church, and to Christ. I don't understand why it is."

" How often do you let in the light of God's Word?" she was asked.

" Oh, I study it occasionally—when I have time."

Her little baby was lying in a perambulator nearby. Looking at the child, he said :

" I suppose you feed that baby whenever you happen to have time—once in two hours to-day, and once in six hours to-morrow, skip a whole day once in a while—just as you happen to feel !"

" Certainly not," she answered, " the child would die under such treatment." And then suddenly she saw the point of the pastor's remarks.

Someone has said, " The dust on your Bible reveals the rust on your soul, and nothing locks the lips like a life that is out of fellowship with Christ."

The Bible is also living in its nature ; it is the incorruptible seed of the Word of God which imparts life in the new birth from above (I. Pet. i. 23).

Here we have no dead literature of a bygone age. Though written by holy men as they were inspired by God many centuries ago, it still speaks, for it is a *living* Word. It is said that Augustine, during the days of his sin and darkness, found the Bible very dull and uninteresting. Later on, however, he was converted, and then obtained the key to the Scriptures. Immediately, the Bible became to him a source of joy and delight.

It is sometimes necessary, in dealing with securities, to place the key of the safe deposit in the joint control of two persons. A divided key solves the problem.

Each person is given half of the key and they must both be present before the safe deposit can be opened to yield its treasures. In seeking to open the safe deposit of God's holy Word it is necessary that there should be the prayerful spirit of the believer, hand in hand with the Spirit of God, who alone can interpret its pages to us; these two, fitting together like the double key, will unlock the rich treasures of the Word of God to the humblest believer.

In Windsor Castle there is preserved General Gordon's well-thumbed Bible. It was his constant companion at all times. In the camp early in the morning, before military duties commenced, a white pocket handkerchief would be seen tied to one of the tent ropes as a signal that he was not to be disturbed for half-an-hour. Both officers and men knew that this indicated that Gordon was perusing that much-loved Bible of his, and was also engaged in prayer for himself and them.

Can we, surrounded as we are with the problems and temptations of life, afford to miss the guidance of divine counsel given through the Bible? "Thy word," writes the Psalmist," is a lamp unto my feet, and a light unto my path " (Psa cxix. 105).

Can we, with so much to discourage us, remain strong in the storms of life without the strength of the Word of God? " Strengthen thou me according unto Thy word," wrote the Psalmist again (Psa. cxix. 28).

Dare we, since the Lord God, the Mighty Creator and Preserver of this universe, and the loving, seeking, saving, Father of them that believe in Christ Jesus, condescended to write His Word to us; dare we neglect it, forget it, spurn it, or reject it? No! with Thine aid, O most Holy Spirit, we will read it, study it, meditate upon it, love it, and obey it. Amen.

Victory Press, Clapham Crescent, Clapham Park, London, S.W.4.